The Persistence Factor

Making Change A Reality Through Persistence

By Kevin Fickenscher

Dedication

To all those who aspire to leadership,
by holding a vision of where to go,
and why,
and who should go with them,
Whose passion sometimes extends beyond the here and now,
but, most importantly...
who want to do right by humankind.

Who also occasionally trips and falls,
or don't reach their initial goals.
But, through drive or passion,
they pick themselves up,
shake themselves off,
and nudge themselves forward
...with persistence...

By using what they have learned
on how to do better,
from all of their experiences.
By revising their course
while maintaining their bearing
By reaching out to gain support
of their fellow compatriots with the same perspective
so, that in fact – they can do better
the next time around.

To those who keep trying
you are offered a tip of the hat,
as well as an embrace
because you now know the way
for meeting the challenges ahead.

It's all about persistence!

From My Heart To Yours

*I wear a small whisk on my lapel every day of the year.
I've worn one every day, on every occasion, on all types
of clothes. And, I'm frequently asked either:*

"What is that, a small whisk?"

or

"Are you some kind of cook?"

My answer is:

*I think I'm a good cook. I love to experiment and actually use recipes as a
"guide" for my cooking. So, I'm just an OK cook. But I wear a whisk
because I tend to stir things up. My wife tells me I stir up trouble. The
whisk is my metaphor for how you make change happen through
persistence. If you stir too fast, you'll make a mess. And if you stir too
slowly, you'll fail to bring things together or burn the meal. But if you
stir just right, you'll bring things together just right. Learning the skill
requires persistence.*

*My perspective is that in life – like cooking – it's important to stir just
right to make change happen!! Just as in cooking, where persistence is
required to become a great cook or chef by serving the very best
preparations, being a great leader who makes change a reality also
requires persistence.*

Persistence is the name of the game!!

Table of Contents

Acknowledgments

First and foremost, I want to acknowledge all those who have worked with me over the years as I slowly but surely attempted to learn and embrace the essential elements of leadership. It's a work in progress. My persistent past is littered with both successes and failures, which have served as the foundation for my education on the core elements of *The Persistence Factor*. As leaders, we often learn over time that one of the most important elements of leadership success is to hold a team of individuals committed to the same goals, working in the same direction, with the same degree of energy to support the required change. Without the support of those around you, making change happen is markedly diminished.

In particular, I would like to mention Tommy "Joe" Johnson, MD, my mentor of many years. He hired me fresh out of residency to develop a "rural health program...*of some sort*" in North Dakota, my home state. I had traveled to New York City – my great escape from the clutches of North Dakota – where I was completing my residency. He, however, convinced me to take the job "to help the people of North Dakota." My brain questioned it, but my heart leaped at it right away. So, I moved back home with true excitement about the new challenge ahead.

I will never forget that on about day five of my new experience, I asked for an appointment with "Tommy Joe," in a fit of panic, who was serving as the Dean of the medical school. His assistant got me in right away. When I showed up, I closed the door to his office and started sharing with him the litany of items I had accumulated on my notepad, when I started to cry from the anxiety of it all. I was totally overwhelmed and felt like I had no idea what to do. He listened carefully. In desperation, I asked Tommy Joe: *What should I do?* And, he very calmly got up from his desk, walked around to where I was sitting and said: *Why don't you go out and ask the people of North Dakota what they want from the rural health program you've been charged with responsibility to create? Ask them. I'm sure they will tell you."*

I took his advice. I visited farmers, local businesspeople, educators, legislators, store clerks, owners, and people I met at local diners, as well as healthcare professionals, essentially anyone who would take the time to talk with me. It was through this process that the essential building blocks for creating a rural health program, wanted by the people, became visible and viable. And, without knowing it, those experiences created the foundation for my learnings on the essential elements of *The Persistence Factor,* which I now share with you...

About The Author

Kevin M. Fickenscher, M.D., is a resident of Maine, where he has settled over the last decade following a wide-ranging career with various domestic and international leadership roles related to healthcare delivery, technology, policy, and association sectors. He continues his work in the field by providing strategic and advisory support related to healthcare with a specific focus on technology applications, informatics, telehealth/telecare services, and leadership/team development. In addition, he has been actively involved in state and national politics for nearly 40 years in a diverse array of roles extending from his time as a national medical student advocate, candidate for office in his home state of North Dakota, advisor to state and national candidates, and other related efforts focused on "making healthcare better" – his self-defined professional purpose in life.

As a result of working in pursuit of his self-defined purpose in life, Dr. Fickenscher has served in various professional roles, including leadership in healthcare development, turnaround, expansion, and redirection initiatives both domestically and internationally. As a result of his diverse experiences, he is recognized as a physician executive leader with extensive experience in strategic and operational development in complex healthcare organizations. He is considered a thought leader in health and healthcare transformation, leveraging the effective application of technology, telecare, information management, and leadership. He holds extensive experience in organizational and societal transformation driven by the digital revolution sweeping across society, as well as physician management, health policy analysis, clinical quality, and resource/care management. He regularly participates in discussions and debates related to the future of the industry, including testimony before Congress and various international healthcare forums. Among his other accomplishments, he has been a Regional White House

Fellow finalist [1984], a Kellogg National Fellow [1985], and an Emerging Leader in Healthcare [1991].

He has a passion for leadership development and has published two books: *The Turnaround Imperative* (1996), which focuses on the need for healthcare to redirect its efforts toward value-based care, and *Toto's Reflections: The Leadership Lessons from The Wizard of Oz* (2013), which uses the story of Oz as a metaphor for leadership lessons. He hosts a monthly blog, The Fickenscher Files,[1] on various topics related to healthcare, politics, and societal concerns. He increasingly enjoys the warmth of the people residing in Maine, along with the shoreline tides that are in constant motion as they embrace the landscape with wave after wave of persistent effort.

A Prologue and Manifesto

"A word about my personal philosophy. It is anchored in optimism. It must be, for optimism brings with it hope, a future with a purpose, and therefore, a will to fight for a better world. Without this optimism, there is no reason to carry on...we must visualize a mountain with no top."

Saul Alinsky
Rules for Radicals

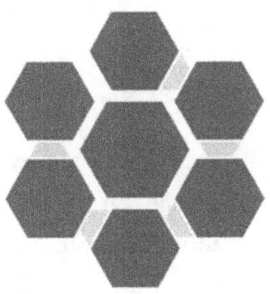

In a word, it seems to me that too many of us have not fully embraced the one perspective that's crucial for sustaining change, and that's *persistence*. During my formative years, like many of us in the 1960s and 1970s, I engaged in considerable dialogue with friends and colleagues about the state of our nation. In particular, the great angst among the American people at that time was due to the ongoing war in Southeast Asia that was reaching its zenith. Not only that, but the war issue was coupled with the ongoing expansion of American economic globalization, which appeared to be disrupting all types of workers.

Furthermore, much like the experiences of today, there were advocates on all sides of all the issues. On college campuses, marching in the streets became a regular phenomenon. Coffeehouses and chat rooms sprang up throughout the nation where intense debates were engaged among friends and foes. Some advocated strikes. Some advocated withdrawal to distant nations. Some advocated insurrection and institutional destruction. Some even took up arms with struggles in the streets, and where effective political discourse was pushed into the background as an austere absence – much like today's world. In a nutshell, change was on the horizon in every direction of societal interaction.

To be clear, I was not an advocate for destruction nor quiescent acceptance as a pacifist either. I felt there was a middle ground where we could come together to "solve" the problems that plagued our nation. I frequently shared my admonition with friends, foes, and colleagues alike by using a metaphor. I would opine:

> *"...we need to learn how to get inside the buildings and renovate them*
> *and not simply tear them down because we don't like their*
> *appearance..."*

Renovation is often much more difficult – and even more arduous at times – than simply destroying something and starting over, especially when applied to societal change. Renovation requires conversation, it requires consensus, it takes time, and it frequently results in delays, but in the end, it will most frequently result in wider acceptance among the populace. But, while it frequently results in the mobilization of fewer resources, it does require *more* time than simply engaging in destruction. But, if adopted, it maintains what was good in a better state while simultaneously discarding what was bad with what can be accomplished...through persistence.

My perspective only expanded when I completed my first biology class in college. I learned that a cell is defined as "the smallest basic unit of life that is responsible for all of life's processes." Cells across the entire portfolio of life serve as the essential structural, functional, and biological units for life as we currently know it. Cells of many types can also replicate independently due to the external influences of other inducer cells. Cells as diverse as single-cell microbes live – and even thrive – in cellular ecosystems. Their survival occurs through the cell's evolution, where it has developed the capability to engage in communal support with other adjacent cells.

These learned cells accomplish their defined tasks through a process of cellular recruitment called induction, in which the differentiated cells produce a signal that drives adjacent cells to differentiate into the same type of cell as the inducers! Essentially, cells send out "chemokines" as invitations for the adjacent cells to migrate and join the inducers. Ah, the magic of biology. Such an approach to cellular survival is one of the mechanisms for cancer to disseminate or spread in the body. Induction can be good, and it can be bad. It was through this biological edification that my perspective on life continued to grow and evolve as I took that metaphor and applied it to the problems we seemed to be experiencing in community life. It became increasingly clear to me that applying the cellular induction concept to the societal problems we face – a much more complex ecosystem – could be successful in driving change.

In many ways, communities and nations function much like the cells we rely upon. We draft our policies, institute our laws, and manage our institutions to maintain the stability of our lives through the process of "induction" by gaining, engaging, and seeking the support of those around us. Similarly to cellular induction, we reside in collectives of individuals called communities, who live and work in the same or adjacent communities. Yet, while the adjacency issue has been challenged in recent years by the virtualization of our personal and professional lives, it is the network we surround ourselves with that helps us create the environment and change what we desire or not. The advent of ubiquitous connectivity has enlarged and broadened our communities as they've gotten larger, more virtual, and more diverse.

If we stop and consider our network, it's increasingly clear that we rely upon our collective for both public and private support, problem-solving, consensus, and for creating some degree of stability related to our perspective as well as the living arrangements in our communities of choice. In essence, like the cells upon which we are based, communities are an accumulation of different cell types gathered together as an organism, where we rely upon one another for support of all kinds. I raise the biology example because my mantra for persistence since those early years of learning about cellular collaboration is that the joint action of working together to solve a problem works better for facilitating lasting change.

And, finally, it was around this period of my life that I learned about Saul Alinsky, who captured the idea clearly with his mantra for fostering change: "Recruit to a cell – a C-E-L-L." Or, his more expanded definition stated simply as: *"...find out what the individual's perspective/interests/desires are and recruit them to your cause based on their needs and desires..."* Through such an effort, the diversity of cells can come together and work together to make our efforts and actions stronger. By integrating and engaging fellow travelers, we can support one another, yielding better results.

If we hold a mission in life...

> If we believe that our chosen approach to work must change...
>> If we see a problem that needs to be fixed...
>>> If we want to alter the direction of society...

We must engage a diverse group of others to join us!

It is through **persistence** and the initiative derived from the perspective of **recruit to a cell** that we can encourage and engage others to join us. And, if practiced in an open, collegial way, acts of persistence represent an effective approach toward making a difference in the lives we touch, on the issues we face, on the directions of society, on our relations with the rest of the world in support of the values and needs we hold dear for society writ large.

So, read on! And, don't forget:

...Recruit to a cell!

CHAPTER I

What Is Persistence?

Come, come, whoever you are.
Wanderer, worshiper, lover of leaving.
It doesn't matter. Ours is not a caravan of despair.
Come, even if you have broken your vows a thousand times.
Come, yet again. Come, come.

Jalaluddin Rumi

A 13th-century international Persian poet universally
acclaimed for his perspective on life.

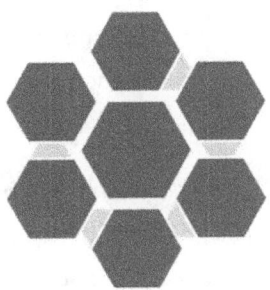

While the idea of ***persistence*** has been around as long as Rumi and most likely, even before – think Moses in the desert with the Israelites – the word was not formally recorded until 1546. Bishop John Bale of Ossory in Ireland, who served as a historian and polemicist, included the word in his writings. The word was derived from the French "persister"[2] and "persistere."[3] In more recent times, the act of *persistence* has come to mean *firm or obstinate continuance in a course of action despite difficulty or opposition,* or *the continued or prolonged existence of something.* When applied to an individual, it is frequently defined as *the quality that allows someone to continue doing*

something even though it is difficult or opposed by other people. Regardless of which definition is used, the focus of persistence is on *making a difference through action,* which, in my opinion, is a simpler and more focused definition.

These definitions imply that the persistent person quite simply continues to work on, to pursue, or to continue engaging in some object of desire despite the difficulty of the pursuit, the challenges, the setbacks, or the opposition by others to their efforts. Furthermore, persistence requires consistent effort or determination in achieving a goal, even when faced with discouragement from obstacles, failures, or setbacks.

In essence, persistence is about staying committed to a course of action over time, without giving up. It can be seen in various aspects of life, such as in personal growth, professional pursuits, learning new skills, or overcoming adversity. It's often considered a key trait for success because it allows us to continue making progress and ultimately reaching our objectives, even when immediate results aren't apparent. To summarize the various thoughts on meaning, it seems that at its core, persistence implies passion and heart, with a touch of bullheadedness.

If we review the thesaurus, several synonyms for persistence pop up for your consideration as well. Words like tenacity, determination, and indefatigability are applied. I think the most apt description of those three words is the utterance by Sir Winston Churchill on October 29th, 1941, at the height of the Siege of London at The Harrow School, where he attended school as a young boy. The Americas had not yet entered the war, which would occur two months later, so Britain was facing the Nazi challenge all alone. A growing sense of dread pervaded the entire United Kingdom. Churchill came to the school and stood on a podium before a small sea of young British boys and, with a loud exclamation of both voice and demeanor, said:

"Never give up! Never! Never! Never!" [4]

You can imagine the resolve that such a statement could infuse among those boys despite the enduring daily conflagration from the barrage of bombings across the homeland. Churchill's statement gave those young lads at the school – and the people of the United Kingdom – the resolve to persevere. The feelings of desperation that were seeping across all of Great Britain during the siege from Hitler's blitzkrieg or "lightning war" across Europe were held like a dam against the destruction as a result of Churchill's statement.

Persistence is partly about maintaining one's fortitude. But we should not glide lightly over the difference between "persistence" and other similar concepts that are part of our lexicon. For example, there is **perseverance** – a word that is closely aligned with persistence. *Perseverance* is originally derived from the Latin *perseverantia,* which means to abide by something strictly. In modern times, it seems to me that perseverance and persistence are too often used interchangeably without recognizing the subtle differences and nuances between the two concepts.

Perseverance equates to continuing on a course of action with *strict adherence* to a requisite set of rules or guidelines. This can make sense in certain situations where a clear path or process is defined as the one way to accomplish an objective or complete a task. Such situations may require you to adhere to a strict set of defined, step-by-step requirements. Completing the construction of a put-it-together-yourself product from Ikea requires perseverance. There is only one way (generally) to get their products safely constructed. Another clear example is learning a new language. It requires perseverance through the use of daily practice. I'm sure you can think of many other examples.

Persistence – on the other hand – requires an investment at the personal level in creating the right environment and culture that will:

1. Allow your *purpose* to unfold,

2. Sustain an individual or group focus on your objectives through your *commitment of time* to discussion, dialogue, and debate on the perspective you share,

3. Facilitate an *open consideration* of all the issues,

4. Foster a distillation of thoughts, perspectives, and ideas to provide a *focus,*

5. Encourage an *ability to learn* from misdirection and failure as a precursor to success through support of your purpose,

6. Support dedication toward *integration of learnings* derived from the full spectrum of experiences; and, finally...

7. Maintain an open dialogue with others as part of a strategic effort to garner support by understanding, appreciating, and addressing the full range of perspectives that impact your initiative.

These seven characteristics serve as the core for defining the requisite path of persistence by creating a repository of personal energy, fostering and supporting passion within yourself, your team, your organization, and your community for facing resistance, disbelief, insufficient support, and other impediments blocking the full embrace or implementation of the ultimate goal. Furthermore, it is important to note that building an environment or creating a culture that includes these elements is a substantially more difficult task in my experience than taking on an Ikea-like project.

The literature is replete with thoughts on how to build an appropriate environment for sustaining persistence. Most of the perspectives come back to a common thread of building trust through the enlistment of fellow advocates. Without trust, the people who work with you will be unable to focus, and they are unlikely to invest the long-term amount of time required to accomplish the initiative. Their energy will dissipate over time, their passion will subside, their dedication will erode, and the initiative will fail.

So, the obvious question is: *How can one build trust so that one can persist?*

I think it starts with the attitude you bring to your environment: how you interact with those around you, how you adapt, the openness you offer to alternatives, the choices you make, your presence in the world around you, the trust you build with those with whom you interact, and how those individuals respond to your choices by embracing your mission.

Pastor Charles Rozell "Chuck" Swindoll, an evangelical pastor, radio preacher, educator, and author from Texas, wrote a poem – "Attitude" – that captures the ideas I'm trying to convey:

> *The longer I live, the more I realize the impact of attitude on life.*
> *Attitude to me is more important than the past,*
> *Than education,*
> *Than money,*
> *Than circumstances,*
> *Than failures,*
> *Than success,*
> *Than what other people think, say, or do.*
> *It is more important than appearance, giftedness, or skill.*
> *It will make or break an organization, a school, or a home.*
> *The remarkable thing is we have a choice every day*
> *Regarding the attitude that day, we will embrace*
> *For we cannot change our past...*
> *We cannot change the inevitable.*
> *The only thing we can do is play on the one string we have.*
> *And that is our attitude.*
> *I am convinced that life is ten percent what happens to me and ninety percent how we react to it.*
> *And, so it is with you...we are in charge of our attitudes.*

So, the message is clear: ***Start with attitude!***

What About Resilience? – Another word that is frequently confused with persistence is ***resilience.*** It's a word that has been bandied about in the literature of late as a differentiator from those words that embody "firm or obstinate..." The American Psychological Association[5] defines **resilience** as "the process of adapting well in the face of adversity, trauma, tragedy, threats or significant sources of stress, such as family and relationship problems, serious health problems or workplace and financial stressors." It is not described as an extraordinary capability or skill, but rather as an element that we all carry to varying degrees. The issue is our ability to adapt. An erosion in our adaptive capability occurs when adversity, trauma, tragedy, threats, or sources of stress persist over time. The breakdown of resilience is, in many respects, the critical factor in precipitating the syndrome of post-traumatic stress disorder.

Not to split hairs, but persistence is the external action taken in response to a situation. In contrast, resilience is the internal adaptation we employ for managing our response to a situation or challenge. The people we work with or those who are part of our teams commonly demonstrate **resilience** if the elements of trust are present, as noted above. At its core, your ability to demonstrate persistence helps build trust and facilitates collaboration with those who share common perspectives. These two elements – persistence and resilience – form a common thread that enables making a difference through their synergistic interaction, as evidenced by our experiences and findings in the literature.

So, it seems that persistence without resilience is, therefore, possible but quite difficult, in large measure because successful persistence requires others working alongside. Persistence without resilience could be considered "bad persistence," where we continue to operate or move forward in maladaptive ways that are not healthy for us or those around us. Persistence can, therefore, be both sustainable or episodic, depending on how we manage the situation.

Sustainable versus Episodic Persistence – Beyond the notions of both perseverance and resilience, the notion of *persistence* without other qualifiers seems to be a rather empty idea. To be firm or obstinate without other qualifiers could result in obstructionist behavior in a world that increasingly values a team mentality.

"*Sustainable persistence*" – in contrast to episodic persistence – is imbued with the values that provide the context and worth of the persistent goal. But the immediate questions that come to the forefront are: What are those values? Who sets them? How have they been defined? In considering the potential qualifiers that could potentially be offered for a more refined definition of sustainable persistence, I considered the great religions of the world. While they can be criticized for numerous issues that have caused difficulties in society, they are also purveyors of a rich set of sustainable values. For example, in the Bhagavad Gita, all Hindus of faith are called to *dutiful action*. Such adherence is considered a very important attribute of individuals who represent themselves as true believers. Similarly, for Christianity, the Bible emphasizes *compassion,* which is considered a crucial value for true believers. For Confucianism, it is *propriety* or *integrity*; and, for Islam, one of the most important characteristics of believers is *humility*. For the Jewish faith, it is "*tikkun olam,*" which translates to *repairing the world*. Despite the differences among various faiths, it is essential to recognize the common threads that unite them, which relate to their enduring presence in society.

Now, I'm sure that the immediate reaction by many readers would be – "Say what?" Any of us could point to individuals or even segments of our society that supposedly espouse the beliefs of these various religions that don't seem to come even close to representing the values I've just laid out. While I don't want this to become a polemic on the religious beliefs of society, I would say that those adherents who don't exhibit the values are either not well-read, don't understand the core values of their religion, or, for other reasons, have chosen to adopt opposing viewpoints. So, the question I wrestle with is: What are the qualifiers? It is in pondering this question that I came to the following perspective:

The Persistence Factor is an approach for creating, supporting, and successfully pursuing initiatives that integrate a set of values with a proactive problem-solving approach for implementing an idea or solving a problem through sustained effort toward reaching the completion of the initiative.

Persistence, by itself, seems rather empty, which is why it requires qualifiers to guide efforts in *making a difference*. One important value underlying persistence is trust. Trust evolves from an attitude that permeates any initiative and serves as the foundation of persistence. Furthermore, as the foundation for persistence, trust is built upon adherence to several key principles. These principles provide the necessary building blocks for sustaining trust in a team. So, what are they?

1. First, an environment of **Fairness** is an essential foundation for everyone involved in your initiative, from team members to the positive and negative stakeholders related to it.

2. Then, exhibit your fairness through the **Attitude** you share with those around you.

3. Embrace these principles with **Integrity** in the relationships you hold with team members and others with whom you interact related to your initiative.

4. From there, you need to offer and foster **Respect** for the perspectives of all those working with you on the team or in the community on the initiative.

5. To maintain the stability of the team or the community, the leader must then offer **Consistency** as a balancing factor in an increasingly chaotic world.

6. Always be open and honest with **Transparency** as a foundation for all interactions among team members or community members related to their ideas and perspectives.

7. Then, circle back to the consideration of **Fairness,** which serves as a core benchmark for building your foundation of trust in the work you do with everyone.

To refine our definition of persistence and make it sustainable, consider hosting a "retreat" with yourself to reflect on the important principles and how you want to pursue them through your work with others. I would simply request that you at least consider these principles as proxies for helping to further define your notion of persistence or, as we will now refer to it, "*sustainable persistence*." You can remember them as "***FAIR Consistency and Transparency.***" So, again, those principles would be:

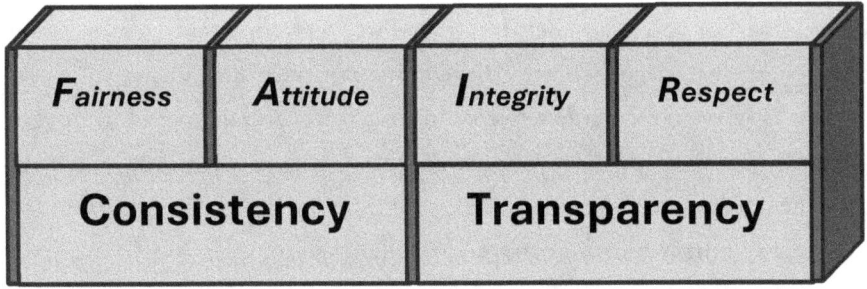

To fully integrate these principles as core building blocks in your approach to sustainable persistence, there is also a need for some mortar to hold these principles together. You might consider taking dutiful action, showing compassion, practicing humility, and focusing on repairing the world. It's your call, but the mortar is an important final ingredient to consider in building your foundation for developing and deploying sustainable persistence.

In addition, it's equally important for you to be clear about your own "personal" values that you carry with you throughout life. They may differ to a degree from those mentioned above. For example, early in my career, I defined a slightly different set of personal values that have guided my approach to work in organizations where I have served as a leader. Those values include: *Responsive* and *Responsible*, *Integrity*, *Creativity*, and *Excellence* (R^2ICE). To drive the point home with my "teams" (across multiple organizations), I have had a tradition of handing out small glass canisters containing "rice" as a reminder of the values they can expect will emanate from my actions and activities in support of the team. The visual reminder was frequently adopted by the members of the team, not only by placing the canisters of rice in visible locations in their workspace settings, but also by members of the team, in like manner, offering rice to those who worked with them. *The lesson?*

Values clarity begets values adoption

A persistent leader who embodies a clear set of values is the type of leader that people will follow. The importance of stated and exhibited values lies in their ability to build faith in a leader's capabilities. The above list may not be the right values for you as a leader. It is, therefore, very important to spend some time engaged in deep, reflective thinking about what constitutes your core values. How are your values reflected in your work with others? How do they present? Are they part of your core? You will find over time that your statement of values will serve as the foundation for building *sustainable persistence* in the work you focus on throughout your career.

The Difference Between Personal and Group Persistence – One of the key considerations in evaluating the characteristics of effective persistence is the distinction between personal persistence and group persistence. Both play a vital role in change initiatives, but they function differently in how they're *driven, sustained,* and *expressed*. It's an important distinction because what drives personal persistence is often different from what drives the persistence of a group.

An Overview of Personal Persistence – The persistence we exhibit as individuals in our personal, professional, and community lives is driven by purpose, conviction, identity, and the values that stem from these attributes. The motivation is an internally driven engine that speaks to us regularly. The motivation provides the vision, meaning, and *sense of calling* that many of us incorporate into our daily lives. It's also often a result of past incidents that *provide emotional connection*s to particular issues we have experienced during our lives.

For example, I've noted in my author overview that I am a physician with a mission to "make healthcare better." It began as a result of a declaration I made in the 6th grade in our school newspaper, stating that I intended to be a "brain surgeon" someday. I'm not sure where that thought came from...but I talked about it a lot when I was young. As I grew older, I got involved in music and theater. My interests then gravitated toward acting. As a result of those interests, I became a member of a singing group in high school as well as the lead in a number of plays that allowed me to share this growing interest. And, through those experiences, I began to consider a career in theater. I was excited...

Until one day, I came home from high school. My Mom, a strong presence in my life (I'll leave it there 😊), said: "Kevin. We need to talk. Sit down!" At that point, I knew we were on the verge of a very serious talk about something she had strong opinions about. As I remember the short conversation, it went something like this:

Mom: "Kevin, you've really gotten into this theater thing."

Me: "Yes, it's exciting and I enjoy it a lot."

Mom: "Well, we need to talk about that because I have some thoughts."

Me: "Well, OK. What are your thoughts?"

Mom: "Kevin, you may think you're good at theater and singing, but you need to know that no one is going to come see you. There's no future for you in theater, so you should give that up right now. You've always talked about becoming a physician in the past. Have you forgotten? Anyway, you need to buckle down and start studying hard so you can go to medical school. Then, you'll have a career where you can support yourself instead of living hand-to-mouth."

Me: [silence] But, Mom...

Mom: "Did you hear me? You need to buckle down!"

Me: "OK."

As a result of the short, kitchen conversation with Mom, I shifted my *personal persistence* efforts! Such a change can occur during the formative stages, when our focus and life goals are not yet well-defined. This is why it is so crucial to be clear about your focus. What are you trying to accomplish? How do you want to apply your personal persistent energies? Where do you want to go? What impact are you trying to facilitate? By addressing these core questions, you can become clear about your personal persistent objectives. And, sometimes it takes a conversation with "Mom," or your "Mentor," or your "Boss," or your "Board," to develop the clarity.

I shifted my ambitions from a career in theater and began the long, at times arduous journey toward becoming a physician, which I do not regret. It is something where I've been able to help people in a direct way and fulfill a desire to "make a difference." The lessons we learn that often emanate from early experiences often serve as the core elements of a framework for *The Persistence Factor*. In my case, my persistent objective became to *"make healthcare better."* And, I don't regret it. After all, no one was going to come and see me at the theater, anyway 😊.

I anticipate that this brief overview of "life with Mom" provides a clear example of how personal conviction, internal motivation, and past experiences with an emotional connection help to drive the foundation for the development of the focus for our persistence. Such experiences create a resilience and mindset of self-discipline and self-reflection that guide us in our search through life. Others may also step forward to help cement personal persistence as well. Mentors can be a valuable resource for supporting and developing our personal persistence. Activities that allow for rest, inspiration, and spiritual renewal can also be factors driving our personal persistence. It is through the strength of these experiences that we can mobilize the personal fuel of life to overcome obstacles, seek careers, raise a family, and the other elements that support our defined mission, despite any potential setbacks that may occur along the way.

However, there is a downside to personal persistence. While we pursue the object of our desire, we may miss the needs of others around us. By constantly working on our careers, we may lose touch with our families. We may also speak truth to power. As a result, our personal persistence may create situations where we are terminated from our jobs because we cannot back away from the itch that drives every moment in life. It can lead to burnout and even isolation. So, a word of caution: make sure you put a governor on your personal persistence motivation. Evaluate it frequently. Accept the feedback of others as you pursue it. In other words, don't be left behind as the train of life closes the doors, pulls out of the station, and moves on without you or others who have joined your persistent effort. And, it's very important to remember the "others" who join us in our persistence initiative because they are frequently the critical difference in making reality happen. So let's consider them.

What Are The Key Elements of Group Persistence? - First and foremost, there is a higher degree of complexity associated with group persistence because it's not all about you. Rather, it's about the collective. Group persistence is driven by the development of a shared identity, a collective vision, and social contracts established by groups as they work, live, associate, and/or engage in life together. There will be more to say about this in later chapters, but group culture is a key element of success in group persistence. It also requires leadership, which can be provided by you as well as others who, with mutual reinforcement of purpose, goals, and objectives, support the persistence objective defined by the group.

Group persistence – unlike personal persistence – requires strong communication and trust among and between the members of the group. Roles and responsibilities can be distributed, but must be defined and accepted by the group. It's also common in group persistence to experience the evolution of traditions and rituals, and to share milestones that become markers for sustaining the energy of the group toward the common persistence objective.

In essence, group persistence requires a coalition of committed individuals holding the same goals that may proceed over months, years, or even decades. Examples might include:

- **Months:** advocating for special policy changes by the state government in how resources are allocated by the Department of Transportation related to road safety.

- **Years:** changing the curriculum of medical schools to extend education beyond the "ology"[6] courses to include training physicians and other health professionals on the effective integration of digital health technologies.

- **Decades:** bringing a new medication to market that assists individuals with weight reduction, or gaining legislation to implement the Civil Rights Act, or creating technology for sending a person to the Moon, or a myriad of other examples...

- **Centuries:** pursuit of a proposed amendment to the U.S. Constitution guaranteeing equal rights under the law for all individuals, regardless of sex (i.e., the Equal Rights Amendment).

Group persistence differs from personal persistence in large measure because the effort extends beyond any one individual. It is driven over time by a coalition of individuals who invest and contribute their time and talents to the common purpose of achieving the persistence objective. There is frequently a rotation of leadership – especially if the group's objectives require a long-term investment of time and talent – to avoid burnout among individuals.

The difficulty with group persistence is that the pursuit or implementation of the objective can suffer if responsibilities are too diffused. There is also the risk of groupthink, misalignment of goals and objectives, and internal conflict that can inevitably arise from group interactions, which can stall the achievement of goals. It is therefore especially important for the group to continually clarify the mission or purpose of the group's persistence objective. A crucial point in understanding group persistence is that the movement should not lose its momentum even when the initial leaders step back or aside from their primary role and/or disengage from the persistence objective. They may continue to believe in the objective but lack the energy to sustain a push toward it. At this point, it truly becomes the group's persistent objective!!

The following table provides a high-level overview of the differences between personal and group persistence for your consideration.

Summary of Key Differences

Element	Personal Persistence	Group Persistence
Fuel	Personal meaning/Fire in the belly	Shared mission/Infrastructure
Risk	Burnout, isolation	Fragmentation, inertia
Power	Depth of passion	Breadth of capacity
Resilience	Inner drive	Collective support
Adaptability	Fast but narrow	Slow but stable
Expression	Quiet dedication/Bold leadership	Sustained effort across people/time

General Characteristics of Persistence – Beyond the values that serve as the foundation of *sustainable persistence,* several core approaches must be applied to the "process" of persistence. Think of these approaches to persistence as the armamentarium that sets it apart from other concepts, such as resilience or perseverance. It has been my experience that these actions help define the methods you will use in developing a philosophy and an applied methodology for your persistent efforts and initiatives. By adopting these approaches, you will be better prepared to move forward in creating *sustainable persistence,* where the principles and values you hold forth come into full bloom.

While these six core considerations and the set of personal values I previously outlined are foundational, it is also clear that you may have certain additional values and principles. It will be critical for you to take stock of those personally held values and principles, as they will ultimately shine through in your work with others and your team members. It is essential to recognize that achieving persistence objectives is rarely accomplished in total isolation. Rather, sustainable persistence requires the involvement, dedication, and support of those around you – if you are to ultimately succeed. Therefore, consideration of the following core activities can help you develop and move the team or community and its committed individuals who believe in the sustainable persistence objective you've adopted and advocated.

Those activities include the following:

1. **Define** – As I noted above, it is very important to define your set of values and understand them as well as integrate the core principles of sustainable persistence. Have a retreat with yourself where you consider all of the options. Engage in a brainstorming exercise where you define not only your values but also what you want to accomplish as a leader and how you want to serve. Make a clear statement, write it down, post it on your mirror so you see it every morning, and – most importantly – continue to consider, evaluate, and integrate it into your life. Finally, consider sharing the values with others that you trust...

2. **Plan** – While much of life and many of the projects we lead will have setbacks or even unforeseen obstacles that block your path forward, it is the consistent consideration of those difficulties within the context of a plan that mitigates those risks by providing a clearer path forward for supporting the persistent pursuit of an initiative. Simply being persistent without direction can lead to a set of accomplishments that are neither valuable nor desirable in support of the ultimate objective. The plan provides the context, and this context keeps us on the path toward the potential for a more successful initiative.

3. **Prepare** – A plan without preparation is simply an empty outline of what to do! I could write a personal mission statement and a high-level "things to do" list for running a marathon, but without preparation, the list is useless. The same principles apply to losing weight, starting a project, or leading a change initiative within your organization. Anyone who has

managed a project knows that setbacks and obstacles will appear. Preparation allows us to identify the resources we need to stay on course. Pursuing a plan without preparation leads quickly to failure, leaving us scrambling to pick up the pieces if we are persistent, or walking away if we are not. It is the crucial ingredient that often makes the difference between success and failure for persistent leaders, teams, or communities. With preparation, we have the resources ready to respond to the chaos. Why? Because preparation means considering as many potential obstacles as possible that may impede your path toward your objectives.

4. **Support** – Defining, planning, and preparing are vital first steps, but without creating support for the initiative within your team to implement it, your ability to delegate resources and define responsibilities will be compromised, even with the best-laid plans. You could even make the argument that, of all the activities, creating *support* for the initiative is the first among equals as a determinant of success. However, there are a few other important activities that facilitate the creation of support, including...

5. **Clarify** – A plan where all the resources have been prepared and support is evident, but where the focus is missing, can go in any direction. It's like the song, *Any Road* by George Harrison, which states in the refrain:

    "If you don't know where you're going,
    any road will take you there."

It's a paraphrase of the exchange between Alice in Wonderland and the Cheshire Cat[7] that captures the essence of the need for focus. ***Any road will take you there***! Without focus:

- Any road may end up expending far more resources than you originally planned for your project,
- Any road may be fraught with more difficulties or problems,
- Any road can divert you for prolonged periods while the rest of the world continues down a more straightforward path, and,

- Any road may ultimately lead you in a direction leading to the demise of the persistent person and their mission as a leader!

After considering all these ideas, it then circles back to...***attitude*** – another very important characteristic of *sustainable persistence* that highlights your determination. As noted previously, attitude is important for building trust with a team. Attitude creates the right atmosphere surrounding your leadership style and the initiatives you propose, giving them a sense of direction. It will also ultimately dictate how others react to your ideas and their response to your persistence.

The quote most often used to describe this characteristic is from Calvin Coolidge, the 30th President of the United States, who was thrust into his leadership role upon the sudden death of President Warren Harding in 1923. Coolidge was a lawyer from Massachusetts who held a reputation as a small government conservative and also as a man who said very little while maintaining a rather droll and dry sense of humor.[8] Coolidge captured the essence of "attitude" toward persistence when he noted:

> *"Nothing in the world can take the place of persistence. Talent will not; nothing is more common than unsuccessful men with talent. Genius will not; unrewarded genius is almost a proverb. Education will not; the world is full of educated derelicts. Persistence and determination alone are omnipotent. The slogan 'Press On' has solved and always will solve the problems of the human race."*

6. ***Openness*** – There are many synonyms for openness, including:

blunt, candid,
    direct, frank,
        honest, forthright,
            open-hearted,
                outspoken, or
                    plainspoken.

In working with teams, I often tell people, *"I'm very direct. I tell people what I think, so I don't have to remember what I've told them. If I change my mind, you can remind me, and I'll accept that too."* This kind of openness is constructive and engaging. Once people understand your clear objectives, they are usually inclined to join your effort, regardless of where the solution comes from. In my experience, this openness among leaders is uncommon but foundational to sustainable persistence.

Openness to new ideas, approaches, and ways of doing things enables a leader to persevere and embrace change. A leader who perseveres without openness risks failure, which then demands different approaches to solve problems. Without openness, leaders remain stuck in what exists rather than exploring what can be. In today's fast-changing world, openness is not only important but essential for success. We can't rely solely on old models. Surviving and thriving in the coming years will likely require modification or a shift in direction. Why? Because the rapid pace of change demands openness to alternative ideas, perspectives, and beliefs – even those that challenge existing models. So, openness is a key trait for fostering and supporting sustainable persistence.

7. ***Attitude*** – Once again, attitude raises its presence as part of any initiative. This part of our persona involves our state of mind and mental position on the information we are assimilating. It is displayed not only through the use of words but also in our bodily reactions, our demeanor, and our responses to the stimuli we encounter in our interactions with others. Attitude is not a characteristic that is easily hidden. Our attitude is woven through and through on the shirtsleeves of our persona, including our entire approach to problem-solving. As a result, without the proper attitude, we can often undermine efforts to initiate or complete persistent objectives.

This brings me to the final activity that is important in *sustainable persistence.*

These seven characteristics of persistence – define, plan, prepare, support, clarity, openness, and, of course, attitude – serve as the mortar for building a foundation whereby all of the principles come together to support building a persistence strategy. By working on and adopting these seven core characteristics related to any persistence project:

- Your ability to overcome inevitable obstacles will be facilitated.
- You will not be perceived as lacking in clarity or be considered indecisive.
- Your strength as a leader will come through for those who follow your lead because they will be empowered to offer critiques or countervailing viewpoints that can even take your organization in slightly different or new directions and paths.

Persistence requires a team working together and harnessing the energy of the entire team to move their common objectives forward. Adopting the seven core activities moves you in that direction.

Furthermore, it is also important to note that these seven characteristics are – for all of us – *a work in progress.* I've learned over the years that I must continuously work on developing my personal capabilities in each of these areas to support the foundation of change initiatives in order to reach for *sustainable persistence.* Essentially, we are all works in progress and will likely remain so throughout our entire lives.

The pursuit of *sustainable persistence* requires a focus on retaining a "top of mind" exploration and evaluation of one's skills and abilities in the areas described above. None of us is perfect all the time. None of us is always an expert in persistence on all issues for all considerations. Maintaining the *characteristics of persistence* is akin to maintaining your car, your career, your friends, your marriage, and your presence in life.

Finally, it is also important to note that while understanding and adopting these core characteristics as part of persistence initiatives supports the how of building persistence, there is a need and willingness on your part as the leader to continuously re-evaluate your values and approaches used in your pursuit of persistence, which is why the cycle of persistence is continuous. Once it seems clear, you must cycle again!! Or, as I have shared with my teams many times...

"The downside of moving too quickly is that you too often proceed without defining your purpose, considering the ideas and perspectives needed for accomplishing your objective, committing the requisite resources, focusing your team, assessing their capabilities; and, taking insufficient time to integrate your successes and failures; before starting the cycle all over again as a continuous effort to resolve and improve your efforts. If you follow this path, you will likely succeed. Go for it!"

Persistence is not static. It requires continuous reconsideration, rebalancing, reevaluating, and redirecting. While the framework of persistence can be considered sequentially, the clear need to engage in a process of continuous recycling is apparent. Such an approach creates sustainable persistence and facilitates gaining support for accomplishing the persistent goals you have outlined as part of your initiative. The cycle includes the following considerations:

Purpose – proactively review and reconsider the focus of your persistent objective. Without clarity on our purpose, we become lost and unable to offer support to the other foundational elements.

Consider – search both far and wide for ideas, resources, services, and capabilities that support the purpose by actively considering alternative ideas and perspectives that may challenge the originally defined purpose, but which in reality offer a refinement that enhances support for your persistent initiative.

Commit – emanates through a process of recommitment to purpose, including any refinements derived from considering alternative ideas, methods, approaches, and frames for implementation.

Focus – is the core for the actual implementation of the mission and/or purpose of the activity, initiative, organization, and/or change that requires persistence, energy, and support to become a reality.

Assess – is the recognition that all leaders, projects, initiatives, and/or organizations must be willing to accept and embrace both the failures as well as the successes related to a sustainable persistent initiative, which means that you must create a sustainable learning environment.

Integrate – the synthesis of the learnings, ideas, resource commitments, approaches, and mission through persistent application of the cycle as a framework for fostering and supporting an approach to persistence that makes life better for people, organizations, and/or nations.

Repeat – the cycle continuously to maximize the value of persistence toward making a difference in the world in which you live. The world needs more persistence. So, keep reading and learn more about what and how it works...

But what about failure?
Isn't failure inevitable on some initiatives?
How does failure result in persistence?
What can we do to mitigate failure and foster success?

Although I'm a big proponent of the notion that persistence, with the right purpose, commitment, focus, and set of values, can capture the imagination and perspective of the community, that's not always the case. Too often, persistence fails because it does not consider the seven essential steps outlined above. Yes, persistence for even the noblest of objectives simply fails by ignoring this cycle of work. So, the question you are no doubt asking yourself is: Why?

First and foremost, I would argue that the persistence objective most often leads to failure on the back of rigidity and stubborn adherence to a singular approach. Your ability to adapt, revise or even change strategies, and learn from the setbacks that will inevitably occur is an important underlying element of your leadership as an effective steward and proponent of the change you are offering. Those who disregard the warning signs of an unsustainable path will end up in a blind alley with no followers. In essence, integrating the lessons learned from setbacks is an essential step in moving forward with your persistence objectives.

And, once you've gone through the process to integrate the lessons learned, reconsidering the path you set for success is an important next step. Actively reviewing alternative perspectives, allowing challenges to existing activities that support a shift or redirection to occur, and modifying the original purpose in response to a changing environment will facilitate movement toward your persistence objective. These are the characteristics of flexibility rather than rigidity that are essential elements as you move through a process of refinement based upon the support of your persistence objective. In particular, we are all captive to the environment in which we live. So, what are some of those warning signs?

- **Economic Downturns** – especially at the macro level – can undo all of the best intentions.

- **Technology Evolution** - As we've seen in recent years, the impact of technological evolution is precipitating massive disruption in traditional environments, which are undoubtedly undoing or disrupting persistent objectives held in certain quarters.

- **International Disruptions** - an obvious disruptive force in an economically interconnected, global environment.

- **Insufficient Resources** - the inability to obtain adequate financial and/or people resources and support is frequently the downfall of well-meaning, persistent objectives pursued by individuals or groups.

However, at the end of the day, these disruptions may only pause your progress if you maintain a persistent perspective as an invaluable and internalized characteristic and keep the cycle constantly in mind. You can make your dreams come true. To make it clear, persistence requires a long view. For example, my life's purpose has been to "make health care better." If I consider it from the short-term perspective, there are clearly failures that have littered the landscape and prevented making that mission a reality. At the same time, "health care" as a product for society is so much better today than it was even

25 years ago due to the ongoing research, dedication, and investment by people and nations.

Therefore, remaining aware of the obstacles, holding a realistic assessment of the current state, remaining flexible, and holding a long view will help you in your mission to accomplish your persistence objective. Remember, even though the following thought came from a movie, not a person, **many of us who pursue long-term goals with persistence and energy hold the belief that *"failure is not an option.""[9]**

Let's move on and fully explore each of those important elements of persistence...that, when supported by working together with others who share the same passion, deliver results!

And, Finally...Why Is Persistence Important? – For starters, persistence is crucial in making meaningful change a reality, whether it's related to personal, social, or organizational considerations. Furthermore, the entire notion of "change" is an interesting phenomenon. It can be viewed as either positive or negative, depending on the viewpoint of the populace affected by the change. The result of their viewpoint is to either embrace or resist the proposed change.

On the following pages, the assumption is that those who are pursuing a persistent initiative are engaged in an effort that benefits the whole, which depends on your particular viewpoint. From a social perspective, let's assume that your persistent efforts are intended to "make things better." If so, your effort needs to understand and address the concerns of those who are resisting the proposed change. Simply overpowering people and the resistance they might offer to a proposed change will only result in resentment and counter-persistence! As you will learn on the following pages, truly effective persistence evolves by:

1. **Learning Through Failure** – because the mistakes and strategic adjustments help to create a focus for moving forward.

2. **Building Momentum** – since it is obvious to most of us that change takes time, with persistent action creating momentum over time.

3. **Establishing Credibility** – through the seriousness of your efforts, the trust derived from your efforts, and the credibility created over time on the need for the change.

4. **Overcoming Resistance** – by continuously reinforcing the direction of the persistent initiative and commitment to change.

5. **Achieving Long-Term Goals** – since significant goals like social justice, climate reform, health care transformation, or other significant changes often require months, years, even decades, and sometimes longer to realize results.

In short, persistence transforms intention into reality. It bridges the gap between seeing an issue or problem that requires resolution and wanting to make a change, leading to the resolution of the problem, to actually making the change happen with the support of those who are affected. Furthermore, effective persistence enables the change to remain stable or intact over long periods, often spanning decades, centuries, or even millennia. Without persistence, even the best ideas remain unrealized.

There are multiple examples demonstrating the requirements of persistence, such as societal change movements related to labor rights, civil rights, the LGBTQ+ rights movement, disability rights, indigenous rights, the anti-apartheid movement in South Africa, and many others. Furthermore, persistence is not confined to social issues. Each of these efforts requires a continuous focus, often over months or years, and even decades of energy directed at solving a problem. Additionally, it is essential to recognize that persistence can also be applied to personal endeavors, such as learning a new language, meeting people from diverse cultures, attending your preferred graduate school, or marrying the love of your life, among many other personal examples you might consider.

To illustrate the concept, consider the following two case studies, which exemplify the essence of the persistent focus, the energy and effort, as well as the periodic shifts required by persistent advocates to effect change within society over time.

Case Study I: The Women's Suffrage Movement – The Women's Suffrage Movement[10] was a multi-decades-long fight in the United States for securing the right to vote for women. It bridged the mid-19th and early-20th centuries. Through activism, advocacy, civil disobedience, legislative battles, and eventual legal victories, women finally gained the right to vote, including the passage of the 19th Amendment in the United States in 1920.

The formal beginnings of the suffrage movement in the U.S. started at the Seneca Falls Convention in 1848 through the leadership of Elizabeth Cady Stanton and Lucretia Mott. They led the effort that culminated in the drafting of the *Declaration of Sentiments*, in which the attending delegates demanded that women be granted equal social status and voting rights in the United States. But then the U.S. Civil War intervened! In the aftermath of the war, however, suffrage advocates had gained some traction but ended up going in several directions with different initiatives simultaneously.

The movement quickly split into two separate initiatives: the National Woman Suffrage Association (NWSA), led by Stanton and Susan B. Anthony, focused on federal change, and the American Woman Suffrage Association (AWSA), led by Lucy Stone, which focused on state-by-state campaigns. The latter group had some success when, in 1869, Wyoming became the first state to grant full suffrage. However, they soon discovered that the two organizations were working somewhat at cross purposes. As a result, they merged in 1890 to create the National American Woman Suffrage Association (NAWSA).

Through their combined efforts, the suffrage movement also gained international attention as well, with efforts evolving in the United Kingdom (i.e., their motto: "Deeds, not Words"), New Zealand (i.e., where women were granted full suffrage in 1893), Australia (i.e. the Commonwealth Franchise Act of

1894), and Finland (i.e., who followed suit in the early 1900s). Throughout the movement, suffragists faced arrest, violence, and public ridicule. Arguments against the suffragists were:

...that women were too emotional,
>...that it would disrupt traditional family roles and values,
>>...that activism in politics was unbecoming of women.

The suffragists, in addition to the public ridicule, often faced violence and arrest in the quest for simple voting rights. Finally, in 1920, women in the United States were granted full voting rights through the passage of the 19th Amendment to the U.S. Constitution. But the fight was not over. The Suffrage Movement sparked broader women's rights advocacy by expanding into workplace rights, reproductive rights, and political representation, culminating in the rise of feminism in the early 1960s and the Congressional approval of the Equal Rights Amendment in 1972.

And, through the many shifts and turns, the persistence factor was at work! The movement continues to this date as women have moved into national and international leadership roles throughout the world, both in government, corporate, and private roles. It's an example of persistence of the highest order as an exemplar for how to make change happen.

Case Study II: Fridays for Future (FFF) or The Youth Climate Movement — In August 2018, Fridays for Future (FFF) evolved into a global climate strike, initiated by Greta Thunberg, a Swedish teenager who began the movement by protesting outside the Swedish parliament. She held a simple sign for all the legislators that read *"Skolstrejk för klimatet"* or "School strike for climate." She demanded that the Swedish parliament take stronger action on climate change. As with many persistent initiatives, it started with one person on a mission. Thunberg's solo protest very quickly gained international attention. It inspired students across the globe to take up the same message in their respective countries by demanding that climate action become a priority, with the movement holding the following goals and objectives that demanded governments comply with the Paris Agreement (2015) by addressing the following objectives:

- Raising awareness about the impact of climate change and the urgency of action required to prevent an international calamity.

- Mobilizing the youth of the world to work toward change through peaceful protest.

- Holding world leaders accountable for inaction on climate change.

So, the question can be asked: How do teenagers who hold very little political power manage to capture the attention of policymakers worldwide? First, they began with weekly school strikes, where students skipped school on Fridays to protest. The students would gather in front of government buildings where policymakers were present. Due to their digital savviness, they utilized social media (i.e., #FridaysForFuture, #ClimateStrike) to coordinate strikes and share information about reactions to their suggestions. While the initial efforts by the students started in Europe, the strikes eventually culminated in global climate strikes by students, peaking in September 2019, when over 7 million people joined the cause! Furthermore, it is important to note that the students approached the climate crisis through nonviolent protest, adopting peaceful demonstrations to maintain moral authority and broaden the appeal of their persistent objective.

The movement started by students has now expanded to include many from older generations who have joined the persistent initiative. Climate change advocacy persists globally today and is expected to continue into the foreseeable future. Through the initial efforts of one tough Swedish teenager, there has been a shift in the global discourse related to climate change. The issues have now evolved into a mainstream issue within many countries, but especially among the youth of the world. Their efforts have elevated public discussion and media coverage related to climate science. And, the persistent objective of the Climate Movement remains a work in progress...

However, it's very clear as this book goes to press that the persistent objective has not yet been realized. There is a considerable amount of further dialogue, debate, discussion, and work that needs to occur before we are likely to come to grips with this major, existential crisis facing the world community. Despite those challenges, the movement remains one of the most influential global initiatives of the 21st century, pushing for a systemic transformation toward sustainability and justice. It's clear that the Environmental and Climate Change Movement, as exemplified by Fridays for Future, reflects the growing urgency and grassroots energy behind efforts to address the climate crisis. While we have a dedicated teenager from Sweden to thank for initiating the effort, many more of us across the globe must become engaged sometime in the 21st century to make a difference and realize the persistent objective – we hope. And, the earlier the better!

Finally, another consideration that affects all of us, in many direct and indirect ways, is the globalization of the human community. In the distant past, we lived as hunter-gatherers, then as wandering tribes, before forming small, distinct communities or aggregating in groups adjacent to communities, which later evolved into nation-states or countries. It appears that these tribal affiliations are now beginning to dissolve economically, socially, politically, and demographically, as we are increasingly interconnected through digital sources rather than physical proximity.

Communications, technology, economics, and statecraft have all become intertwined. The interconnections are now at a point where, in many different ways, we rely on one another across borders, geographies, and political lines for daily sustenance in our lives. In such an environment, a persistent approach becomes an essential ingredient for the successful collaboration and integration of ideas related to the pursuit of goals, aspirations, initiatives, projects, or whatever you intend as your persistent objective.

Therefore, let's move on to a framework for pursuing a persistent objective that holds the potential to gain the backing, support, assistance, and energy of the majority for the benefit of the whole...

First, There's
Purpose

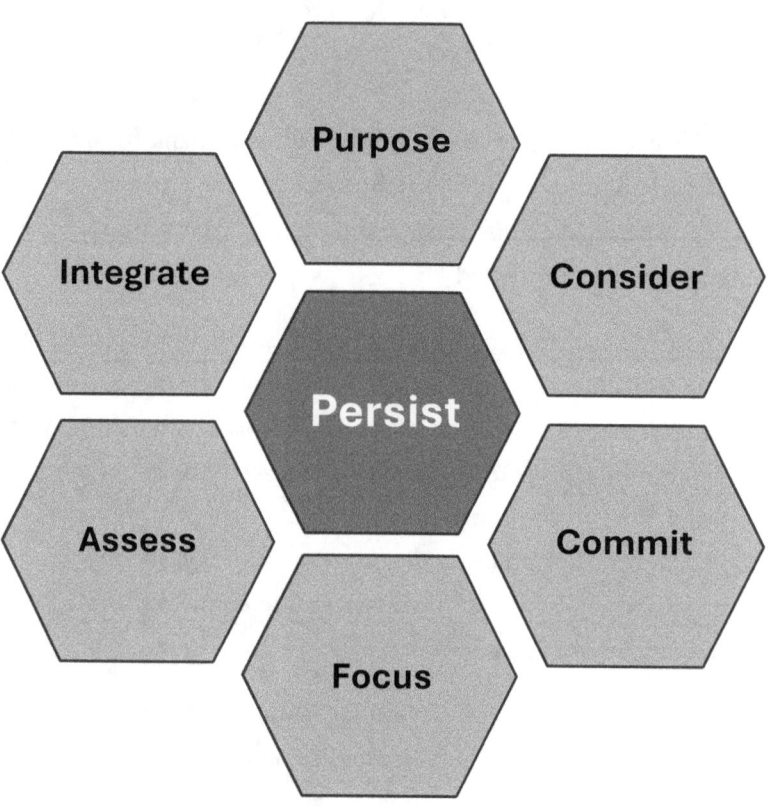

CHAPTER II

How Our Purpose Evolves: A Framework

Persistence without purpose, plan, path,
<u>and</u> presence will simply be perceived as pushiness.

Kevin Fickenscher, MD

...a student of leadership
who continues to learn about life

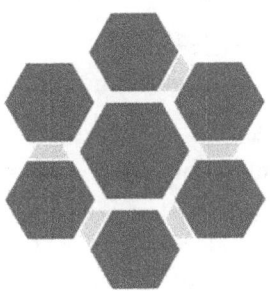

Much has been said about the need to have a purpose in life. As we become older, the sense of *purpose* becomes even more of an issue for most of us. For myself, that sense of purpose has tended to follow the stages of my life. And it seems that, as I commiserate with many of my friends and colleagues, they are experiencing the same phenomenon. Furthermore, as we bring closure to one stage, a new, ever more enlightening stage seems to open up.

What do I mean?

Looking back, the early years and adolescence were preoccupied with *exploration*. Whether it was exploring our bodies as very young babies when we seemingly marveled at our ability to point our fingers or feel the warmth of our mom against our skin – we were exploring ourselves in the context of the universe we inhabited. Exploration continued as we grew older and ventured beyond the immediate purview of our parents and other guardians.

Outward exploration even meant disappearing behind the garage or hiding behind a tree so that we seemingly disappeared, only to pop out at the last minute to "scare" our parents, who were calling out our names. Exploration also meant extending the reach of our kingdom beyond the confines of our immediate locale by venturing down the street or walking a block or two away from the safety of home as part of exploring and expanding the world in which we lived. Reaching outward, expanding our world, seeing how things work – these are the key elements of exploration in those formative years of life.

And the exploration continued into the adolescent years, where we often explored areas that may be defined as "verboten" (German for forbidden) by Mom and Dad, or ideas that were simply not allowed to be discussed, whether it was drugs, sex, or any other unmentionable topic. Many of us as adolescents explored, some with abandon, but most with caution. These experiences represent the fundamental building blocks for the foundation upon which we build our perspective on...

Who we are...

What we want...

And how we proceed...

...in gathering our requisite needs at that point in our lives. Through those adolescent experiences, we initially frame our approach or seminal personal model on how we view persistence or not as it relates to all aspects of our lives. Whether it's managing school, interacting with classmates, dealing with a bully on the playground, expressing our first love, or whatever context we find ourselves in, we are truly exploring.

Toward the end of the adolescent era, we make a subtle shift in our journey. Whether it is through the chiding of friends or the cajoling of family, the notion of "When are you going to make something of yourself?" comes into play, or, at least, that was a major theme in my household and for many of my friends. Such a focus represents a shift from self-exploratory work toward a focus on our *potential contributions* to some portion of the world around us. Common questions for this period are:

- What are you going to do when you grow up?
- What do you want to make of yourself?
- What comes after this?
- And, so on...

The shift towards the contributory element of life redirects our focus away from the self towards the external world, often embodied in terms of professional pursuits. It is at this point that the purpose we hold forth is no longer about ourselves but about some goal or objective we articulate for our friends and family:

- I want to be a farmer just like my dad, my Grandad, and my Great-Grandad!
- I'm getting ready to apply to university.
- I'm going to be a doctor. No, a neurosurgeon!
- I want to be a police officer.
- I intend to be an expert on the application of artificial intelligence in management.
- I want to act in a play on Broadway!

These represent the "*professionalization*" of our purpose. Purpose becomes imbued with all the attributes and characteristics of a projected life, often by others rather than yourself. I describe it as "projected" because, at this stage of life, when our purpose emanates from outside of us rather than within, the foundation is often not as strong. We may have ideas, wishes, or desires that percolate outward, but these can become deflected by circumstance,

by family,

by culture,

by a whole series of externalities over which
we have little, or at least, lesser control.

As a result, many of us proceed down a path with dogged determination, focusing on a path laid out by the dreams of others, often a path laid down for us before we have even arrived on the scene. To be that doctor, we need good grades in certain fields, but not just good grades. We need good grades in calculus, biology, and chemistry. A list of "shouldas" serves as the focus for our purpose at such a point in life. And, as a list of prescribed activities required for supporting the purpose set forth by others, it represents a formula of: Meet-these-goals-and-your-objective-will-be-achieved. Yet, we ask ourselves: Is it?

It is at this point that the inherent capability for building true persistence comes into play as an increasingly important part of our lives. Happenstance is put aside, and a truly persistent focus begins to take over – one that creates us, drives us, and, ultimately, defines us. This initial stage of true persistence development is quite nuanced. Our purpose most often becomes more than simply an individual quest. It becomes a journey that is accompanied by others who have joined us in life – our spouse or partner, our children, the people we meet at work or in school, our extended family, members of the community, and others who decide to become part of our circle of life. This stage goes far beyond the professionalization of purpose to the *personalization* of purpose.

The personalization of our purpose is a period that extends over a much longer period than the previous stages of growth and development. Rather than a mere decade or two, an ingrained purpose may well go on for many years through all of the ups and downs of our lives as we persistently pursue our purpose. It is the stage when we call upon ourselves and frequently others to contribute toward the path we have selected:

- I intend to help those with fewer resources than I have so they can build a decent life.
- My community needs me to be the best teacher I can be.
- I want to help those who cannot help themselves.
- I want to make health care better.
- I want to be a millionaire.
- And, so on...

During this stage, our **path** is reset, at least for some time, by activities that lead us toward achieving our plan, so that the **purpose** we've defined for ourselves comes alive with energy and focus. Throughout this entire process, persistence is a key factor in determining whether we can ultimately define a set of goals that meet the standards of our family, friends, colleagues, and ourselves. Happenstance can remain a potential deflector or accelerator, but only for a certain amount of time. Through persistence, the purpose you've established for yourself will find a way to infiltrate the obstacles of life, so that you *will* find a way around the obstacles and through the bramble bushes of life! Afterall...

Purpose – more than vision – is, therefore, the cornerstone of persistence.

Vision without purpose is simply a dream.

Persistence without purpose lacks direction.

But, always remember...

Purpose with a vision that follows a direction can change the world.

A Parable[11] – In many respects, stories are a much more powerful modality for conveying the essence of a message. While data, charts, and information have their place in making a point, in considering "purpose," a story is often a much more powerful approach. So, I offer the following story as a metaphor, which, while seemingly close to the story of the prodigal son, is actually based on the "Dakota Vision Quest" – a process used by the Lakota Native American tribes who resided in the North Central regions of the United States where I grew up in growing and developing leaders. The story offers a lesson focused on the need to define our purpose in life...

Once upon a time, there lived a very wise tribal leader who served a small village out on the prairies of a land called Dakota. He was widely respected for his unbiased approach to complex problems. He was also an honest leader who was always fair – and, because he was fair, his decisions were sought by tribes both far and wide.

So, it was with some consternation that the wise tribal chief became increasingly concerned about his eldest son, who he anticipated would step into his role as the next chief of the village. He was concerned because everyone in the village kept observing that his son was a rather lazy person. He always had an opinion but never listened. He did not seem to recognize the contributions of the tribal members toward sustaining the village, nor their needs as the seasons changed. Rather, he simply hung out with a few friends in the forest near the village. He wasn't involved with the other young men in hunting for food for the people of the tribe. He often slept in and expected food to be ready when it was time to eat. And, at the end of the day, when he returned from the forest to join the tribe's campfire, he continued his idle conversations with friends.

The chief had tried tender counseling, admonishments and even punishment and threats – all to no avail. The son would not change his ways. As the years passed, the unrest in the village continued to escalate. Many were concerned about the future of the tribe once the chief stepped aside. The chief desperately wanted his son to assume that role. But, the tribal elders were beginning to share offhand comments and discussions in the fields about their concerns about the future of the tribe. So, the chief eventually recognized the need to intervene in his son's misadventures.

First, the chief consulted with the tribal elders and considered several options. Then, one day, it came to him! It was time for his son to do a

Dakota Vision Quest (a Hanbléčeyapi or "crying for a vision" in the Lakota language). So, he called his son to the family campfire one evening for a one-on-one conversation and said, "My son, you are no longer just a child. You must learn to take responsibility and understand life. I want you to find the real purpose of your life because when you find your purpose, it will serve as your North Star on the horizon for your approach to helping the tribe."

The son listened quietly without response. The chief continued, "Knowing your purpose in life will help you to lead a life full of happiness and joy, not only for yourself but also for those who depend upon your leadership." Then, he handed his son a bag. The son took the bag and held it, unsure of what to do. His father said, "Open it."

When the son opened the bag, he was surprised to see four pairs of clothes, one for each season of the year. There were the heavy comfort coverings of buffalo robes for the winter snows. There were the leggings and gloves for the cool nights and rainy days of spring. There were the short coverings for the hot summer months and another set of leggings for the cooling period of fall, when the animals went into hibernation. The bag also held food grains, some lentils, a few precious stones and a map. His wise father continued, "I want you to go find a special treasure. I have drawn a map of the place where the treasure is hidden. You need to go, find the treasure, and bring it back to share it with the tribe."

The son loved this idea of a new adventure. He was bored with simply hanging out in the fields and letting the days slip into the night. The very next day, he organized all the supplies his father had gathered and set out on a journey to find the treasure. Over the coming days and weeks, he traveled quite far across many borders, through forests, across plateaus, and over mountains. The weeks turned into months with each day bringing a newfound experience. Along the way, he met many people from diverse backgrounds. Some of these people helped him with gifts of food, while others offered him shelter. The people he met taught him new skills and openly shared their knowledge of the lands where they lived. And, along with all of the good folks he met, some caused trouble. On several occasions, he was even confronted by bandits who tried to rob him. But he did not succumb, and he kept his focus on the quest and journey his Father, the tribal leader, had set for him.

As the seasons began to slowly change, along with the landscapes and languages of the people he met, he soon realized that the world where he had grown up was only a small portion of the total world around him. He began to understand that the tribe his father led was also but a small group among the many with knowledge and understanding of the surrounding territory. When the weather turned unpleasant, he would halt his travels, stay in his camp, and reflect on all the encounters he had experienced over the previous months. And when the weather cleared, he continued his journey by building on the experiences he had accumulated along the way.

Finally, after a long year of travel, he reached the place of the treasure marked on the map. It was a cliff. The map showed that it was placed just below the edge of the cliff, seemingly under a tree growing on a small embankment at the side of the mountain. As he surveyed the embankment, he spotted the tree. He then carefully climbed down to the spot and began to dig the ground. He searched and searched – around the tree, under the tree, beneath its roots, even up on the branches – but found nothing. He spent two whole days looking and digging for the treasure. By the third day, he was so exhausted that in exasperation, he decided to leave.

At this point, he was deeply disappointed that the trip had ended with nothing to show. He felt that his father had lied about the treasure. So, he decided to head back home. On the return, he experienced the same changing landscapes and seasons. But there was a difference this time around. Why? Because he halted to enjoy the blooming flowers and watch the dancing birds who savored the monsoons. He stayed in places to watch the sunset over a particular horizon he had neglected to enjoy because he was pressed for time. And, he really enjoyed the pleasant evenings.

Since the original supplies he had been given were now gone, he even learned how to hunt and to cook a good meal on an open campfire. His clothes had become a bit tattered from the trip, so he asked someone he met along the way to teach him how to sew his clothes. He even learned to build small, temporary shelters to protect himself against the winds and storms, as well as the wild animals that roamed the prairie. He also learned to determine the time of day by observing the sun's position in the sky and the direction to travel based on the location of the stars.

He even met a number of the same people who had helped him earlier. So, because they were friends, he stayed a few extra days and helped them with their projects as a small token of repayment for their support during his prior travels through their territory. He shared the stories about his trip and some of the lessons he had learned from his journey. He realized how fortunate he was to have met these people who had taken him in as a stranger. They were incredibly nice. After all, he was just an ordinary passerby who did not have much to offer them except his assistance on their projects.

So it came to be that after many months, he finally reached home after nearly two years' travel away from his tribe. Upon arriving home, he was greeted by all of the tribal members, including the elders. Everyone was curious as to what he had found. But, he felt obliged to first share his thoughts with his father – the tribal leader. So he walked straight to his father's hut. "Father," he said. And, immediately, the wise tribal leader jumped to his feet and hugged his son before anything else could be said. His father asked excitedly, "So how was your journey, my son? Did you find the treasure?"

"The journey was fascinating, Father. But forgive me. I wasn't able to find the treasure. Maybe somebody took it before I reached the place you marked on the map." When he spoke the words, he surprised himself. He realized that he wasn't angry with his father. Instead, he felt bad that he had been unable to find it and return home with it in hand. Instead, he paused and asked for forgiveness from his father.

The father stood there for a moment. He then held out his hands and said, "Son, there wasn't any treasure in the first place." And, he offered a big smile of a proud father.

"So, why did you send me to find something that wasn't there?" he asked.

"I will surely tell you why, but first, you tell me. How was your journey? Tell me all about it. What did you learn? Did you enjoy it?" The son shook his head back and forth, saying, "Well, Father, I didn't enjoy the first part of the trip – or so I thought when I first passed through the lands and the villages I visited. I was too worried that someone else would find the treasure before I did. I was in a hurry to reach the cliff." He continued, "But, even though I did not find the treasure, I really did enjoy the journey – especially on the way back home. I met a lot of people, made many friends, and witnessed the miracles of nature every day."

"Son," the father interrupted, "what do you mean you witnessed miracles?" The son continued, "Well, the sunrises and the sunsets were absolutely incredible out there on the prairie. And, I learned so many new and different skills. I learned the art of survival on the prairie. And then, there were the people I met. They taught me so much. They offered their knowledge of the surrounding area and the best paths to follow to reach the cliff. And, more importantly, they opened up their homes to me, shared their food, and offered me comfort. There was so much I learned from the trip from all of those experiences that I almost forgot the pain I experienced in not finding the treasure."

The father said to him, "Exactly, my son. You have learned well. I wanted you to have a goal and to keep it in front of you, where you were headed. But, I also wanted you to realize that if you remained too focused on the goal to the exclusion of everything else going on around you, as well as the people you would meet, you would miss the real treasures of life. You seem to have discovered the importance of listening to the people who shared their knowledge with you, to learn the lay of the land, to appreciate the support you were given during the journey, and to remain humble throughout this first trip of your life. While it is important to have a goal and to keep it front and center, it is even more important to appreciate all the experiences and knowledge that surround you every day of your life. Without the support of those around you, the goals are merely directions on the horizon. As leaders, we must learn from others. And we often learn best when we help others and are with others, who help us grow every single day. That is how you become a wise tribal leader who is respected by the community.

He paused, extended both hands and said: "You are ready, my son. I am proud."

The parable reveals a path toward defining our purpose. The story makes clear that *defining one's purpose precedes the setting of our vision* as the cornerstone of persistence. It reveals quite clearly that vision without purpose is simply a dream. Rather, persistence is about creating reality for our dreams.

CHAPTER III

Considering Your Purpose

"The purpose of life is not to be happy. It is to be useful, to be honorable, to be compassionate, to have it make some difference that you have lived and lived well."

Ralph Waldo Emerson
poet, philosopher, and leader in the 19th century
on the Transcendentalism movement

The moral of the parable in the preceding chapter is clear. Leaders must learn from the world around them. If they come to their positions or roles with all the answers suddenly imbued from on high, they are simply messengers of the deities in their life and not a leader of their own life. The world is a field with many, many deities or even deities-in-waiting in the vast majority of the organizations, communities, or other places where people gather, congregate, and work.

Our purpose, therefore, is often a distillation derived from the *integration* of all those prior experiences we capture and hold dear through the exploration, the professionalization, and the personalization in which we engage. Our purpose evolves from the accumulation of all those life experiences coupled with *learning*.

What is interesting about this sequencing of persistence is that for many of us, we also reach another state that is much less defined. It's a question that has been haunting me for several decades now, and it comes from a song by Van Morrison where, in his own evocative way, he melodically asks the question:

> *What do you do, when you get to the top,*
> *and there's nowhere to go?*

Well...I've concluded that even at the pinnacle, we must persist!! In a similar thought to Van Morrison above, philosopher Friedrich Nietzsche described in his book, *Twilight of the Idols*[12]:

> *If we have our own why in life,*
> *we shall get along with almost any how.*

So, What Are The Hows? Persistence is a state of mind that we must adopt and integrate into the essence of our purpose in life. Why? Because it serves as the foundation for the 5Ps of a leader's life, including plans, paths, professionalization, personalization, and presence with those we seek and engage in our lives. Also, please note that alliteration serves a point! It's a way to remember the essential building blocks of your Persistence. It is not about pushing aside or rolling over others. Rather, it consists of an intentional dialogue we must have with ourselves as we establish the principles that define us as individuals. These principles become clear as we engage in an internal dialogue and include:

Personal Persistence	Group Persistence
Who am I?	*Who are we?*
What do I stand for?	*What do we stand for?*
Where should I focus my time and energy?	*Where should we focus our time and energy?*

Personal Persistence	Group Persistence
Who needs to be involved in helping set objectives and priorities?	*Who needs to be involved in helping us to set objectives and priorities? And, why would they consider becoming involved?*
When do I start?	*When and where do we start?*
How will I engage the world?	*How will we engage and involve the world?*
How will I accomplish my goal(s)?	*How will we accomplish our goal(s)?*

Sustainable persistence within the context of answers to these seven questions will guide you in ways that allow you to contribute to the greater good while simultaneously nurturing your requirements. It's a "both/and" premise. Furthermore, persistent purpose can be big or small. However, regardless of size, it requires not just a definition but also a plan and a path. And it requires your **presence**. Other words that come to mind that might be equally applicable are bearing, comportment, aura, or dignity. These are all words that imply "a part of," not something "apart from." The distinction is very important. Too frequently, in both professional and personal renditions of who we are or project, the essence of what surrounds us and how we interact with those experiences is often lost. Persistence that loses a sense of what is both personal and professional can obscure our purpose with a perceived degree of pushiness.

John W. Gardner, the founding Chairman of Common Cause and a leader among leaders, often opined that it is a rare and high privilege to help people understand the difference they can make not only in their own lives but also in the lives of others, simply by giving of themselves. He also challenged the people he would meet by asking the question, "What have you done that you believe in and are proud of?" That is the type of question that gets you to think, to consider, to contemplate – your purpose.

Lighting the *fire in the belly*, stirring your passions, and sustaining your energy are some of the critical elements in defining your purpose. At the core of these issues is the need to answer the *"why?"* question. Answering this question is one of the most important cornerstones of our lives as we develop our true persistence. If we have no idea *why* we are moving down a certain path or following a course of action, at the end of the day, we are likely to end up anywhere rather than somewhere. However, by understanding our internal *why*, an inner peace can percolate continuously within us, helping us to persevere even in the worst of circumstances.

As far as we can discern, the sole purpose of human existence is to kindle a light in the darkness of mere being.

Carl Jung

A Swiss psychiatrist and psychoanalyst who founded the
idea of analytical psychology

The other reason that answering the why question is so important relates to the fact that persistent people generally have a goal or vision that serves as their underlying motivation and drive for engaging in the work they focus on as part of both their personal and professional lives. Persistent people also possess a degree of passion that sustains their energy and provides them with a sense of a higher purpose than simply moving deck chairs to earn a living. Passion comes from deep inside and becomes ingrained in us as a force for focusing our energy, direction, and focus.

In fact, among persistent people, there are frequently multiple points of passion that represent some of our first thoughts in the morning when we awaken into the dawn of a new day. These points of passion can be both professional as well as personal. However, we need to become clear about our purpose and revisit it on a regular basis.

Refining Your Purpose – A sense of purpose extends far beyond the professional and often-overlooked personal aspects of life. This very important point was shared with me years ago when I was encouraged to hold a retreat with myself...

to reflect...

to consider...

to contemplate...

to embrace...

a purpose for my life! ***You should do the same!!***

The idea that was implanted in my soul was that if I wanted to identify and retain my purpose as an essential foundation for meeting the challenges and opportunities that would undoubtedly evolve in the coming years, it would be important for me to hold a retreat with myself. I accepted the challenge and visited a retreat center where I sat and considered the questions outlined above, or, more poetically, how I could *kindle a light in the darkness of mere being*. It required time alone to think hard about my options...to write them out...to revise them...to contemplate them as a real foundation of what and how I wanted to be in life. In retrospect, it is the most important process I used in framing my life's decisions on where and how I would focus my initiatives, my career, and my life. And, at the core of those considerations, my sense of purpose was the key factor, with the following added qualifiers:

- What were the important elements I wanted to keep at the forefront?
- Where would I focus my time and energy?
- Who were the other people that I wanted to consider bringing along for the ride of a lifetime?

An important point with this process, however, is that we must recognize our sense of purpose is not static. The important elements of my purpose at the age of 40+ were on family and career, and vastly different from my *evolving* purpose at age 70+, where I hope to continue making a difference but in alternative ways. The reality is that we all evolve. And our purpose evolves as well. As a result, it is essential to periodically revisit our statement of purpose. We need to pull it out, host another retreat with ourselves, and recommit. Without recommitment, our sense of direction for persistence will most likely become lost in the morass of events and activities that come at us each and every day.

And, we need to keep our sense of purpose at the forefront of our thoughts. For example, when I get up in the morning, one of my persistent thoughts on the professional side is that I want to "...make health care better." It has been a part of my passion lexicon for many decades, starting when I was an undergraduate in college. Virtually all of my professional experiences have revolved around this singular point of professional passion for nearly five decades.

But, I also look at the mirror over the sink in my bathroom every morning, where I posted my *revised* "Seven Essentials" about a decade ago. They are a modification or revision of those activities that drive my purpose as I move into the elder years. I even carry them on a card in my pocket every day. I offer them as exemplary thoughts for how you, too, can define your "Seven Essentials" that support your purpose in life.

Number One: *Sustain and enhance my relationship with S* [my wife].
Number Two: *Engage in regular exercise.*
Number Three: *Maintain my mental agility.*
Number Four: *Contribute my knowledge and expertise to good causes.*
Number Five: *Engage in spiritual exploration.*
Number Six: *Develop and nurture "local" friendships.*
Number Seven: *Engage in writing and reading (e.g., books, poetry, etc.).*

What I'm trying to make clear – through "too much sharing" – is that persistence is the integration of several areas of focus, both personal and professional. Having these discussions with yourself is one of the most important elements for creating a focus of persistence for your life and the lives of others with whom you share your life. I still have my "projects" that support my original purpose to "make health care better." But, I've also temporized a bit as life has moved on...

In my case, I review those "Seven Essentials" every morning when I arise. I actually read them. I consider them. I think about them. And I recommit to them when I read that list – each and every morning. It's an activity I didn't engage in earlier in my life. And I wish I had because over time, it has become clear that I am evolving, and so my list must change. As I've continued to reflect on where I was at each stage of life, my purpose, while retaining a primary focus – has evolved. The process of a daily review is an important approach toward sustaining our purpose. Purpose does change over time for all of us for a variety of reasons that are often very personal in nature. We need to accept and embrace it.

In essence, my message is that the internal purposes of our lives, not the external ones, are just as important as we stop and consider how we will engage the focus of our persistence into the future. Furthermore, by being clear on both the external and personal sides of our persistence, we can embrace and balance the persistent objectives in our lives across the spectrum from personal to professional to community...and beyond.

Such is the power of purpose.

One's purpose is not simply a work thing. The power of purpose extends its tentacles through and throughout our lives by providing the connectivity of all that we engage in – both personally and professionally. It is worth the effort to become clear with yourself about your purpose in life. It will help you reach your goals and keep you accountable by serving as a focal point for your daily activities, including the following points:

- With whom do you share your purpose and focus?
- What activities support the purpose you've defined for yourself?
- Where do you want and need to place your energy?
- When should you lead and when should you follow?
- How do you invest your time and evaluate your results?

Getting clear on purpose is the fundamental stepping stone for establishing your persistence quotient. The daily self-reminder of that purpose will help you to consider how best to focus your efforts and energy as you move out to *seize the day.*

So, in the end, persistence without purpose has no path, and we can wander in any direction. And persistence without presence leads to irrelevance over the long term... But persistence with purpose provides the strength of a foundation for one's life.

Take Time to

Consider

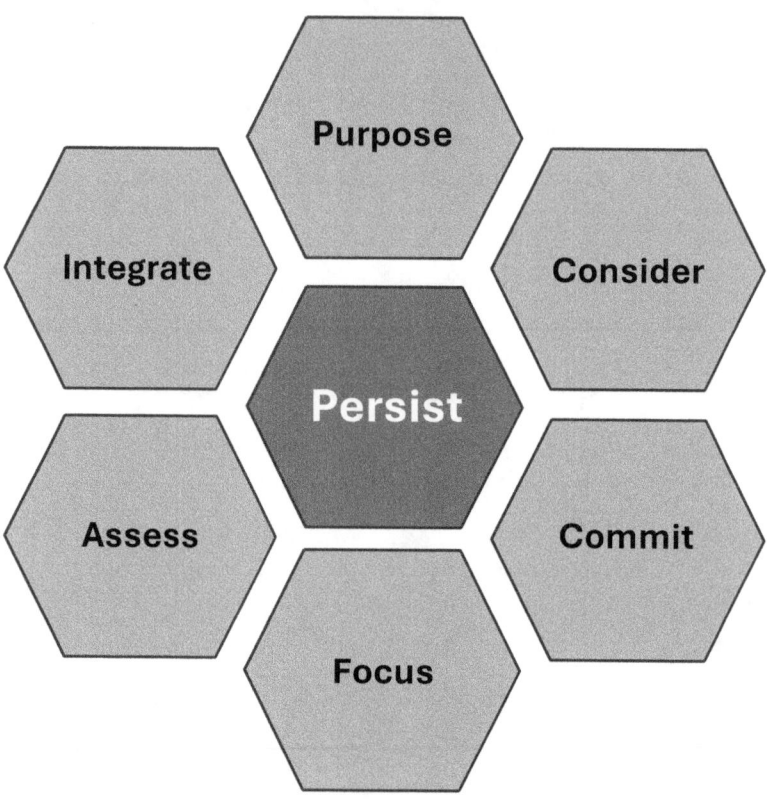

CHAPTER IV

Considering the Requirements for Sustaining Persistence

We must dare to think "unthinkable" thoughts. We must learn to explore all the options and possibilities that confront us in a complex and rapidly changing world.

J. William Fulbright

American politician, academic, and statesman who represented Arkansas in the U.S. Senate from 1945 to 1974 and creator of the Fulbright Scholars Program to develop and foster mutual understanding, support, and peaceful relations between the United States and other countries.

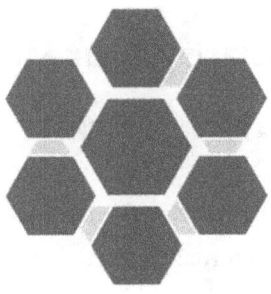

Becoming Clear Through Consideration – I suspect that most everyone who has picked up a copy of this book realizes that "we" – writ large – are facing a multitude of challenges across all societies. From local decisions on how we want to educate the next generation, to funding for our governments, to creating an equitable society, to establishing effective and ongoing international relations, to climate change, to whatever issue sparks your imagination and energy – and, beyond! At the global level, we – the people – seem to be facing a plethora of issues affecting our ongoing relations in an increasingly globalized and interdependent community – or, at least that's my perspective. How do we manage that change? Who will lead the discussions? Will it take persistent efforts to facilitate an effective interconnected state for the global community?

Regardless of whether or not you agree with that last statement, the number of areas requiring the focus of human intellect, talent, and energy is staggering. The level of involvement required for our participation ranges from local to national to international – and, perhaps in the not-too-distant future, the intergalactic realm as well. In essence, there are lots of opportunities for you to focus your "persistence" energies. The question arises: Where to start? To "consider" a project or direction in life that meets your personal needs as well as the needs of society is about evaluating options, assessing feasibility, and aligning decisions with personal values, skills, and long-term goals. The following structure is offered as a way for engaging in those considerations so that you can then "commit" to a course of action.

Step 1. Clarify Your Motivation

Too frequently, many of us bypass the critical task of self-reflection to define very clearly our personal values in reference to the life we lead. It is a task that is often bypassed due to family or external pressures and resources. As a result, we don't listen to our own internal needs and evolving requirements to guide our lives and energy. However, those individuals who become clear about their personal values, what motivates them, and how to integrate that information with their ongoing investments of time and energy will be light years ahead on this front. I encourage all readers to sit (over a period of time, not just at one sitting) and contemplate the values that are important to you. Also, recognize that the values you define may change over time as experience and life become further resources for advising us as individuals on the values we hold for the time we spend in our lives. A clear set of values is an important first step in considering all aspects of your life...

...Who should be involved in helping you with value implementation?

... What will be the focus of your life investments, and what impact do you hope those investments will have on your life or the lives of others, both close and distant?

...Where should you be placing your energy?

...How should you evaluate opportunities vis-à-vis your values?

...When should you re-evaluate your values?

...And any other questions you believe are important!

Once your initial set of values is defined, you need to determine how they align with your ongoing interests and passions, which will ultimately determine how you *commit* to them. Clarification of values also requires that you search both far and wide for ideas, resources, services, and capabilities that support your values by considering alternative ideas and perspectives. Such an approach may challenge the originally defined directions you set for yourself, but will simultaneously offer the opportunity to refine your initial set of values as an initial process of personal persistence.

Step 2. Search, Gather, and Assess

The first consideration under Step 2 is to engage in some research related to how your defined values and passions can be best achieved. This phase will require some degree of research and exploration related to the opportunities that could potentially meld with your values and desired directions.

Not only should you consider talking with people with experience in the areas you've defined for yourself, but also reviewing studies, books, or online resources to gain insights on areas that are synergistic with your defined values is an important part of the process. Furthermore, becoming clear on your strengths and weaknesses that align with the defined values and directions you've set for yourself is important. What gaps do you identify that need enhancement or filling to fully meet the challenges of the areas you've chosen?

It is at this point that you can take an assessment of your strengths and weaknesses relative to the goals and values you've outlined. Next, define as clearly as possible the obstacles that lie in front of you and your team based on those assessments. Through this process, you can define more clearly what it will take to meet the challenges and commit to the longer haul with persistence. Why persistence? Because it is unlikely that opportunities, solutions, approaches, and the like will simply fall into place. That would be the exception rather than the rule. The question that remains is: How do you assess your strengths and weaknesses? You need to consider them by using some available tools that guide your consideration.

Step 3: Assessing Your Strengths and Weaknesses

During the formative years of my career development, I was introduced to the Myers-Briggs Type Indicator (MBTI)[13], an incredibly useful tool for helping someone to understand themselves by providing a scale of their attributes that range from Extroversion (External World) to Introversion (Internal World), Intuitive (Gut) to Sensing (Data), Thinking (Cerebral) to Feeling (Emotional); and, Perceptive (Open) to Judging (Demarcated). For those unfamiliar with the Myers-Briggs, it was developed by Isabel Briggs Myers. Originally, it was a parlor game that Isabel and her mother, Kathyrn, used to describe people they met. Then, during World War II, the tool was discovered and used by the military to accelerate those who might make better pilots with a high degree of success. However, I don't want to get into a big description of MBTI development here. Instead, I encourage you to explore the numerous excellent books on the tool and its applications in support of leadership. The information on this tool has been a remarkable resource for me in my career, and I encourage you to consider using it as a tool to guide your team's development.

My introduction to the MBTI came in medical school when Isabel met with the leadership of the American Medical Student Association. We were so taken by the tool and Isabel that we created the Center for the Application of Psychological Type. Several studies have been done on the characteristics of successful physicians in various specialties. We used the MBTI as a tool to help students understand those attributes and to assist them as they pondered, for example, whether or not they should go into radiology, a highly technical and frequently solitary specialty (my opinion 😊) versus family medicine, which requires broad, general, open-ended skill sets based on their typology. But, rather than get into a long dissertation on the MBTI, I encourage you to consider some excellent resources and references that can assist you in looking at your strengths and weaknesses. In particular, the Center for Applications of Psychological Type[14] is a good starting point for exploration of the MBTI.

There are also other valuable tools in the marketplace. The DISC[15] is a very valuable tool with a slightly different focus than the MBTI. It focuses on the individual's skills but from a different vantage point. In general, the DISC focuses on team performance, productivity, and communication. As you can imagine, the use of "teams" is increasingly how work gets done. And...teams are dynamic. Sometimes you work with the same people for a set time, and at other times, the composition of the team is dynamic and changes frequently. In each situation, a strong understanding of team dynamics will make a difference in how you can function both as a leader and as a team member. Again, a long dissertation is not needed here. Instead, I recommend exploring the DISC for a comprehensive overview of how it works and how understanding team dynamics can benefit you as a leader.

There is a lot of information about positive thinking, both online and in print. The basic rules of positive thinking are to highlight your strengths and successes and to learn from your weaknesses and mistakes. This is a lot easier said than it sounds. We often dwell on attributes that we are not happy with from our past or in our daily lives by making them bigger issues than they need to be. These negative thoughts can be very damaging to your confidence and ability to achieve goals.

You can go a long way by fully understanding your strengths and weaknesses as a point of self-awareness. As the saying goes, *"Know thyself."* For example, over the years, I've learned that one of my great strengths relates to strategy and understanding the dynamics of markets. In some cases, I'm early in my predictions – some might say too early – but accurate, nonetheless. My weakness relates to the operational details of making my predictions a reality for the organization with which I'm working. It's not that I don't understand the details; it's just that I don't find it stimulating. So, I've always, always, always had as my sidekick in successful initiatives an operations-oriented leader. I rely upon the operations person to help me keep the trains running on time and budget. Understanding your strengths and weaknesses is a critical knowledge set that you can develop on your own through conscious self-assessment.

Step 4: Review the Risks & Challenges

Any type of change initiative will present itself with inherent risks and challenges, plus *opportunities*. Once you have a good grounding in your capabilities and approach toward problem-solving, it will be important to determine the potential obstacles to reaching your persistent objective. While failure is a possibility for any initiative, the important consideration relates to the potential implications for you and your team. Questions that need to be addressed at this point include:

- What are the potential obstacles that will serve as barriers toward blocking your persistent goals or objectives?

- How should the potential for failure be assessed? By what measures? And, what are the implications?

- How prepared are you and your team to manage the inherent uncertainty and setbacks that will inevitably arise while pursuing a persistent objective?

- What external support is needed to facilitate accomplishing your persistent objective

- What is the commitment level? Is the team excited or on edge?

- Have you identified the necessary fiscal and personnel resources required to pursue your goal?

- What training and/or education do you and the team need to meet your goals?

- What are interim objectives and/or goals that will facilitate reaching your long-term persistent objective?

- Upon reaching the persistent objective, have you identified the necessary requirements for creating a sustainable, long-term solution?

- Beyond the logic standing behind your goal, what does your intuition or gut say about the initiative?

Step 5: Set a Timeline and Make a Decision

With all of the preparation you and the team have completed in the prior step, you come to a point where you need to make a Go!/Maybe-Depends?/No-Go!!! Decision. This is the period that can be the most frustrating. You have accomplished all of the above and now need to make the final push to allocate resources and engage others in your campaign. It can be a bit overwhelming, but it remains the important final step in moving forward toward accomplishing your persistent objective.

However, once you've gone through each of these steps, it will be important to

...turn the corner,

...face the future, and

...move on to the next big step in proceeding to make your persistent objective a reaiity!

Then It's Time for

Commitment

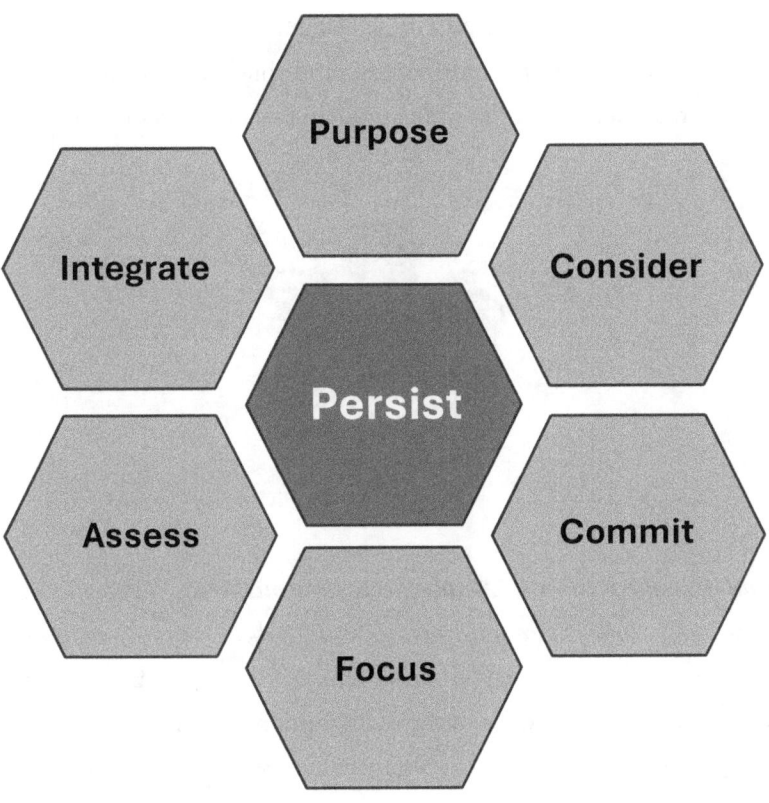

CHAPTER V

Moving To Commitment

Unless commitment is made, there are only promises and hopes;
but no plans.

Peter F. Drucker

whose writings contributed to the philosophical and
practical foundations of the modern business corporation

Beyond Consideration – Moving To Commitment — Peter Drucker is correct that "*...unless a commitment is made, there are only promises and hopes...*" However, suppose you are unable to define the best avenues for accomplishing your purpose and the many options for making it a reality. In that case, the path you choose may not ultimately be successful. It is, therefore, an important exercise to consider all the potential directions in which you can invest your time and talents to accomplish the purpose you've defined for yourself or the organization you serve.

It's also important to recognize that the process of *consideration* is an evolutionary exercise that requires repeated review and, in many cases, "reconsideration." As you gain further knowledge, consider the evolving data, and engage others with alternative perspectives, you are likely to find different and, in some cases, radically different directions for accomplishing the purpose you've defined. Furthermore, while *consideration* is an important process that must be built into dialogues and debates for organizational direction, it is especially important at the personal level. It is also important to remember that *consideration* is built on a foundation of purpose. The greater the clarity of purpose, the easier the path of consideration!

For example, many of us consider a career as the primary focus of our attention for defining our life's purpose. By having clarity on that particular component of life, we believe we can set a direction for sustaining our future. It is also a direction that often captures the family's attention. In my case, early on in the 6th grade, I announced I was going to be a "brain surgeon." I have no idea how that came about, but it got the attention of my parents and other relatives. That idea I brought home in the 6th grade then morphed into "becoming a doctor." Now, I'm more focused on simply "making health care better."

Perhaps an anecdote will help to illustrate the evolution of commitment through consideration. In the formative years of my life, after moving to North Dakota from Nebraska, I learned a valuable lesson from a very important person in my life: my high school biology teacher, Jack Moreland. He had a profound impact on me as a young teen when I overflowed with high ambitions. In my high school, most of us who were interested in health careers took biology. It was one of the obligatory lessons that seemed important on the path to somewhere in healthcare. As part of his biology class, we had both an experiential component and a didactic portion. As I considered a potential career in medicine, I wanted to be assigned to one of the doctors in our community during the week. Even though I had worked as an orderly at a local nursing home and the local hospital, I had never been allowed to "see" how physicians worked outside of the acute care institution, except when I was sick.

Mr. Moreland made the arrangements, and I followed the local pediatrician for a couple of afternoons. It was a great experience. I not only had to engage in the experiential piece, but I also had to prepare a short report on what I had learned and schedule a one-on-one session with Mr. Moreland. The privilege of being allowed the opportunity to follow the pediatrician around made me more excited about becoming a doctor. And, as you may recall from my commentary earlier in the book, I also had a hankering for acting, but that lost out to medicine due to the combination of my mother's intervention and the important experiences that Mr. Moreland arranged for me. As a result, in my one-on-one with Mr. Moreland, I exuded excitement and confidence about the glamor of becoming a doctor. He listened very patiently and quietly. And, when my excitement settled down a bit, I said, "So, what do you think?" He looked at me with all seriousness after a quiet pause and offered the following advice that I will never forget: "Well, if you don't settle down and stop talking about it, and instead start studying, you'll never make it."[16]

At that moment, I was deflated — and quickly challenged! The process of consideration is like that. One moment, we are sure of the direction and approach toward the investment of our time and talents. Next, someone comes along and challenges us with thoughts, perspectives, and ideas that prompt us to pause. It is part and parcel of the process of consideration.

As I sit here and write these words, I'm smiling at his wisdom. I walked out of his room, shuffled to my locker, grabbed my books, went on my way to work as an orderly, and made a resolution to myself that I would study. I would make it into medical school. I would show Mr. Moreland (and my Mom). Sometimes persistence raises its head this way. We are challenged. And our response to the challenge is to arch our backs and move ahead. It requires us to carefully listen to what's been said to us, to absorb it, and to make it part of the persistence equation. Persistence is the mortar that holds our bricks of experiences together in the wall of life...

In essence, what I'm suggesting is that reflection, *continuously over time*, is an important process for building the foundation of our commitment. Let's move away from the personal to the organizational. It is equally clear that the "single offsite retreat" – while important – is an insufficient activity for building a foundation to move a commitment forward. Reflection on the discussions and debates, determining the depth of passion among the team, providing clarity on how the various activities will support the accomplishment of the stated goals, and being honest with ourselves on the depth of our reserves (especially as we age) are all essential building blocks for making our purpose a reality.

The Essence of Persistence through Commitment – While I could recount many stories of persistence, one of my favorite stories of persistence relates to our son, Michael, a notable musician with a growing reputation for Eastern and Mediterranean-style music, as well as folk and jazz. One day, several years ago, I recall working in our home office, which was located upstairs, off a hallway overlooking a downstairs room from the balcony. I remember this one day very distinctly when I was participating in a whole series of back-to-back conference calls interspersed with responses to emails and the usual cacophony of my "work" in the upstairs office.

At some point, however, I noticed a stream of music emanating from downstairs. It was during one of the breaks in my conference call onslaught that I stopped my hurried activity to listen to the musical notes drifting up from downstairs. I remember putting aside the papers on my desk and turning my cell phone off to simply listen. I listened carefully. There was a certain melody that was being played, replayed, and replayed yet again – over and over and over.

However, after listening for a short period, I turned the cell phone back on and went back to my work for another round of calls. Then, another lull in the work activity occurred an hour or two later. What struck me immediately as the quiet in my office overtook my prior activity was the persistence of the tune I had heard emanating from downstairs earlier in the afternoon. It was the replay of the exact same music that had been playing previously that caught my ear again. I found it peculiar that the music emanating from downstairs was the same melody tickling my inner ear. And, I wondered why?

However, the callback to my work took me back into the confines of the office again. I quickly fell back into the work-a-day routine before once again coming back to the continuous melody floating up from below. It was at this point that I remember going to the balcony and listening for a short period before quietly stepping halfway down the staircase. I watched for more than just a short period as Michael played the same set of notes over and over and over again until he got them exactly right! He was nudging himself along toward the perfection of that melody. At that moment, it became clear to me why he was becoming such a well-regarded musician. He was committed to perfecting the musical presentation. It is that type of commitment that prefaces our ability as we seek certain objectives through persistence. Without commitment, persistence cannot become a reality. And, commitment occurs because of the consideration we've given to the purpose of the work or life we are building.

Over the last several years, I've come to appreciate Michael's commitment to his music in ways that go far beyond simple professional or personal persistence and my admiration of his talents. When he plays, he becomes one with the music. Such a state is pure artistry! It is persistence taken to its highest state – commitment. We all could learn much by watching Michael practice. He works so very hard and is paid so very little for a slice of perfection that is the result of his ongoing commitment to offer the very best that he can to the people who listen. It is this type of commitment that ultimately drives persistence toward the success we are all seeking if we endorse the elements of *The Persistence Factor*. Purpose, Consideration, and Commitment – all fit together. But, there's more...

There's also Nudging...

What About Nudging? – So, what is it about Michael that is different from many of us who purport to hold a personal or professional commitment? It appears that the primary difference lies in the nudging process. So, what is nudging? The classic definition of a nudge as defined in the Merriam-Webster Dictionary[17] is "to touch or push gently (i.e. "...*nudged* the cue ball with the tip of the cue" – Paul Theroux), to seek the attention of by a push of the elbow (i.e. "...*nudged* Ron in the ribs and pointed at Malfoy" – J. T. Rowling); or, to prod lightly, urge into action. It can also include the process of prodding (someone or yourself), drawing someone's attention to something, touching or pushing gently or gradually, such as "the canoe nudged the bank"; and, coaxing or gently encouraging someone to do something desired by the Nudgee; such as, "we need to nudge the politicians in the right direction."

In the classic sense as defined by Thaler (a behavioral economist) & Sunstein (a prolific academic lawyer) in their book, *Nudge,* the authors argue that both conscious and unconscious processes are associated with nudging. Their argument is based on the fact that all of us hold biases and quirks that can be predicted. The authors go one step further, however, by noting that if the social environment can be changed, people can be "nudged" toward a more rational behavior, which they refer to as "libertarian paternalism." The example they provide is the state of Illinois' application of a change in the driver's license renewal process to facilitate organ donation. Drivers were asked if they wanted to be organ donors as part of their renewal process. The very act of asking people about the organ donation issue at the time of driver's license renewal dramatically increased the rate of those signing up to participate. That's an example of nudging. The idea is to engage in nudging that can be used with people to uncover ways of encouraging their behavior to move in certain directions that are predictable, both from a conscious and unconscious perspective.

At the practical level, the authors mentioned above, along with others, have applied nudging theory to the realm of politics. We can see the nudge factor playing out in the politics of the last couple of years, but that is a very deep abyss, and we would likely not find a way to climb out...so, let's not go there. Instead, let's shift to a notion that I refer to as self-nudging. As Thaler and Sunstein[18] have defined the idea of a *nudge* as:

"...any aspect of the choice architecture that alters people's behavior in a predictable way without forbidding any options or significantly changing their economic incentives. To count as a mere nudge, the intervention must be easy and cheap to avoid. Nudges are not mandates. Putting fruit at eye level counts as a nudge. Banning junk food does not."

While nudging in the classic definition can exhibit these attributes when applied to us as individuals, I believe the "nudge" required in commitment is quite different. The nudge is derived from an internal source – a place of the heart or mind – that is apart from both the conscious nudging we experience and the external nudging we get from others. The inherent, internal nudging that emanates from deep inside of us is derived from our commitment to a particular cause, idea, or purpose. It's frequently not on a list anywhere – unless one engages in the exercise I described earlier – and it is not necessarily one of those self-imposed requirements we ascribe to for further development of our expertise, knowledge, or capabilities. Rather, it is part of who we are – our commitment.

Much like Michael's practice, through the inherent nudges of practicing his various instruments, he has slowly but surely continued on the road of improvement in style, capability, and talent. It is his commitment to music that stands out. The same concept could be applied to...

- The committed surgeon who masters a set of very difficult procedures to become a pre-eminent technical provider because she has the inherent nudge of wanting to do the best job she can for her patients;

- The architect who can blend structure with the environment in such a way that the combination of the two creates a captivating blend on the horizon;

- The teacher who, through his persistent commitment, devotion, and time allocated to children, can convince them to not only complete their education but excel in their chosen field, even though they come from a disadvantaged household;

- The politician who focuses her time on a singular set of issues that together help to redirect the investments and programs of government at the state or national level, because she believes our society must resolve inequities in resource allocation and distribution.

These are a few examples of inherent nudging supported by one's commitment to a particular consideration. Many different examples could be applied to the concept of the *inherent nudge*. Think of yourself, for example...

What is the inherent nudge in your life?

There is a considerable body of literature on the concept of nudging, and most of it relates to politics and economics. How can we *nudge* someone to vote for a certain candidate or a certain amendment? How can we *nudge* a young millennial to purchase a particular product? Or, a boomer? How can we *nudge* or convince a segment of the population that a position taken by a legislative body is correct? And what is the best way to nudge them to get on board? Through social media? Advertising? Face-to-face sessions in home districts? The list goes on and on... Here a *nudge*, there a *nudge*. Everywhere a *nudge*, *nudge*!! Hopefully, you can see the *nudge* at work in your world now that I've explained it!

What About Mentors? – Whether inherent or not, nudging is derived from many different motivators. Some of us need the motivation of someone looking over our shoulders to keep us on track. Others need interaction with someone we highly respect to discuss our activities, plan of action, and review of results. Which, in essence, is the role of a mentor. Mentors can help us find our path forward in the river of life. They can help us steer our craft to skillfully navigate the most treacherous waters. They can advise us on the types of supplies we will need and how often we will need to seek additional provisions for our long trip. Mentors can be an invaluable resource for helping anyone not only to define their commitment but also how best to execute it and continue on the path forward.

As I consider my career, my mentor, Tommy Joe, has been an essential partner since I began as a budding physician following my residency. Not only did he provide guidance, but he also was known on occasion to give me a "whack upside the head," followed by the emotional support of a surrogate father. And, as a model for what I could become, he provided a path I could emulate.

As reported on a management and mentoring website that finds mentors for individuals, there are five critical roles mentors play[19] in helping mentees grow and develop. They include:

1. **Serving as a Teacher**: Through their modeling behavior and information sharing, they can assist the mentee in better understanding what is needed to solve the issues they are facing, both personally and professionally.

2. **Serving as a Sponsor:** This involves helping the mentee by opening doors so that they can further develop and augment their talents, as well as identify areas in need of augmentation.

3. **Be the Cheerleader on the Sidelines:** We all need inspiration from time to time, and an effective mentor can provide the energy and support we need for achieving our objective at hand, as well as challenging our assumptions about the problem and providing encouragement as we search for solutions.

4. **Provide Effective Counseling:** The mentor can also serve as an essential "counselor." An effective mentor listens, probes, suggests, clarifies, and advises as a neutral third party to the ongoing discussions we frequently have with ourselves.

5. **Be a Friend:** We all need friends who are willing to take our calls at any hour of the day or night for any reason to talk through any issue. But also, beyond the strong mentor who is a friend, the need for a strong cadre of friends is important as a resource for unbridled advice for sustaining our persistence in the face of adversity.

Even with all of these external supports, we need to realize that commitment is an internal drive. While outside support and motivation can help create a burning desire, we all need an internal engine of commitment to maintain our daily lives as we face inevitable failures, blind alleys, and times when progress seems glacial in its pace. These are the times when inner energy becomes a critical resource for maintaining our commitment, serving as a foundational element of persistence.

Finding, identifying, and nurturing that source of energy is one of the more difficult tasks, and it will not happen amidst the multiple demands of our daily lives. Instead, to gain a personal perspective on the source of your commitment, you need to spend time with yourself, which can be both a difficult and an enlightening experience. I encourage you to pursue that course. And to keep them front and center...

Take notes.

Generate ideas.

Share them with your mentor.

Paste them on the wall.

As an example, I noted earlier in the book that nearly a decade ago, I typed up in large 24-point font on a single piece of paper the "Seven Essentials" in my life. I pasted them on the mirror in the bathroom so that every morning when I arise. I also carry them in my pocket so I can look them over and again embrace them throughout the day, as needed. They are a critical resource in reminding me what is important in my life, why I do what I do, and how I spend my time. Consider it. It's simple, and it's present at the start of every day and in my pocket all the time. It reminds me of my persistent goals in life. Encourage yourself. Stop and be with yourself, which is probably the most powerful activity in which you can engage. Consideration comes first, but commitment will be the result...

Next Comes

Focus

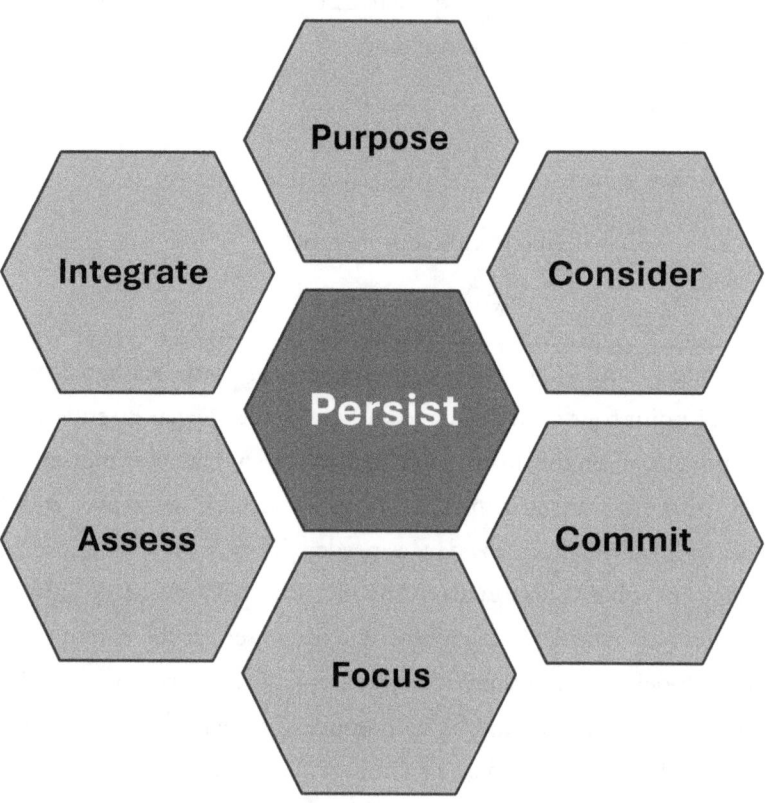

CHAPTER VI

Focus Derived
From Confidence and Tenacity

*Always bear in mind that your own resolution to succeed
is more important than any other.*

Abraham Lincoln
16th President of the United States

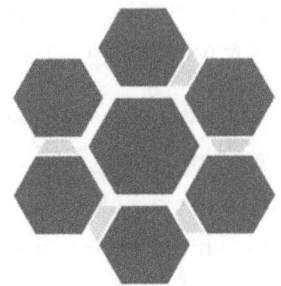

First, An Exemplar of Confident Leaders – Many leaders can be highlighted for their capabilities and focus on making a difference in their community, nation, and world. However, certain iconic leaders often demonstrate persistence as a key element of their leadership in a broader sense. From my perspective, Nelson Mandela is such an iconic figure of the 20th century. His stature and impact on the world are exceeded by very few people. He ranks alongside Winston Churchill, Mahatma Gandhi, Rachel Carson, Franklin D. Roosevelt, Rosa Parks, and Martin Luther King Jr. as individuals whose commitment made a lasting *difference*. When we examine their contributions to society, we learn that their commitment was made after reflection, discussion, and debate with themselves and others on the directions that needed to be taken for solving a problem, seeking a solution, or raising awareness. Furthermore, their commitment evolved over time.

While each of these leaders stood for commitment, Mandela's story is particularly compelling. He was imprisoned for decades because of his stance against apartheid.[20] His journey began when the South African National Party – a whites-only government – established the policy of apartheid in 1948. It was shortly after that that the opposing African National Congress (ANC) committed itself to the overthrow of whites-only rule, and Mandela was appointed President. He then became prominent for his involvement in the 1952 Defiance Campaign and the 1955 Congress of the People. Following these two events, Mandela was repeatedly arrested for sedition, but he was unsuccessfully prosecuted until the 1964 Rivonia Trial, when he was charged with conspiring to overthrow the state and sentenced to life in prison. In facing the death sentence, he made the following statement to the Court:

> "I have fought against white domination, and I have fought against black domination. I have cherished the ideal of a democratic and free society in which all persons live together in harmony and with equal opportunities. It is an ideal which I hope to live for and to achieve. But if need be, it is an ideal for which I am prepared to die."

Other individuals show evidence of focus as well. While the Greatest Generation[21] offers a diverse portfolio of leaders who exemplify focus and tenacity, there is no doubt that another leader sits atop the list as a *leader of leaders* from the 20th century. Sir Winston Churchill has been described as one of the most capable leaders of his time and of history, where his ability to manage all manner of problems or difficulties was exemplary. He used the force of reason and his will to gain the advantage over others, and it all started in his younger years as a student at St. George's boarding school in Ascot, Berkshire. He was known for seeking out a life that lived on the edge. At an early age, he demonstrated a knack for political life through his skill with words and his understanding of the classics, as well as their historical context. He did not excel at sports or math, although he "got by," so to speak.

But more than his contemporaries at school and beyond, Churchill learned his limitations. Rather than accepting them, however, he reached out and challenged himself to do better, to learn more, to try harder—all traits that would bode well for him in the future. He excelled at diversifying his talents by painting and building a garden outside his home, all the while honing his political skills and capabilities.

It is the confidence that he cultivated throughout the world that became the essential foundation of his leadership during the challenges of World War II. Of the Allied leaders, Churchill stood head and shoulders above them all. His confidence spread among those leaders by creating sustenance for continuing onward during very tough times. His confidence was built on a foundation of unparalleled perseverance, mental energy, and physical stamina. Through his presence and continuous connection to the people of London and the English more generally, Britain was able to withstand the Blitzkrieg that decimated the buildings but not the spirit of the British people.

And yet, Churchill was not described as an arrogant leader. He was confident. He was centered. He believed in his mission. And he exuded a contagious quality to onboard people to the goals he set forth. What does it mean to be a confident, persistent leader? It means you must hold beliefs that are centered on reality – a reality that can be challenged but that is palpable and centered, nonetheless. It means you rely upon others to help and guide your efforts – the experts, the other leaders in the same boat, the trusted confidants who continuously feed you both good and bad news, as well as those whose ideas may seem on the edge but in reality, are right for the situation. In other words, no one is closed off. You listen and interact with everyone who can help you to lead.

Churchill laid it all out very clearly before the House of Commons in November 1939, when he stood before his fellow leaders as the First Lord of the Admiralty and stated with resolve:

"In the end, we will break their hearts. We shall suffer, and we shall suffer continually, but by perseverance and by taking measures on the largest scale, I feel no doubt that in the end, we shall break their hearts."

The Work Of Building Confidence – At the outset, let me be clear: building confidence is not an isolated activity. It is not an attribute that is acquired and then set aside as an accomplishment. It is a work in progress - continuously! Rather, confidence is a process that requires a *positive state of mind*, continuous *training* and practice, knowledge about the areas in which you are engaged, and the ability to communicate effectively. It is the feeling you get when you successfully merge these four attributes as you work toward solving a problem, considering an issue, or making a point of change with others. How does one go about building self-confidence? After all, I suspect that if we could bottle it up and put it on the market, we'd sell a lot of it.

First, it seems to me that to build one's self-confidence successfully, we need to understand the origin of why self-confidence might be lacking. The literature is clear that there are many factors that contribute to a lack of self-confidence, including:

- the criticism we receive of our performance or our *outward appearance,*

- *feeling unprepared* for the situations we are placed in because the right information is not available at the right time,

- *prior failures,* which can tend to feed on themselves by creating new failures if appropriate self-interventions are not pursued,

- *lack of context* on the information or knowledge about a particular subject matter for which we are being called upon to offer an opinion or lead a discussion,

- *low self-esteem* for whatever reason – whether internally driven or outwardly generated; and,

- allowing *extraneous distractions* to pull us away from focus (yet another chapter ☺) on the "right stuff."

You can see that there is a bit of circular discussion here. Engaging in the right activities fosters self-confidence, while a lack of investment in those activities leads to a lack of self-confidence.[22] In essence, it is important to support the side of the circle that develops your capabilities. Let's take each of these areas and discuss them in a little more detail.

Managing Criticism – As a very young man, I had a difficult time managing criticism coming from my fellow schoolmates. I was called "Giraffe" because I was tall, gangly, and uncoordinated. Many a comment was made – clearly within earshot – that, "Oh, he's just a giraffe." It was disparaging, and I remember one day finally talking with my Dad about it. He – like me – was a tall guy, but he carried himself well and was very respected by folks across the spectrum of the community. We had a lengthy discussion, and although I don't recall the exact content, I do remember what he did. He handed me a copy of Dale Carnegie's *How to Win Friends and Influence People*. The book had a profound impact on me. As a young man growing up, I probably read the book every year until I started college. I was even so presumptuous as to give it to my eldest daughter and son one Christmas. I remember their incredulous looks as they unwrapped what I thought was a wonderful present. I quickly concluded that one needed to be at a moment of needing the information conveyed in the book to fully appreciate the value of the gift.

Regardless, the power of positive thinking is an incredible force for improving one's confidence. The power of positive thinking is derived in large measure from a rational approach to the problems you face. You need to understand your strengths, appreciate your successes, and learn from your weaknesses and mistakes, which is a lifelong process. Too often, when we confront major problems or seemingly insurmountable tasks where our notion of success is not the outcome, we focus on the result. Instead, to be successful in building self-confidence, you need to corral those negative thoughts about why you failed and instead focus on how you could have done it better so that the <u>next time</u> (and there is always a next time), your chances of success are increased.

Prepare and Plan – Too frequently, leaders will forge ahead with support for an important implementation initiative without putting in place the proper tools and resources. Whether you are considering a new job, taking on a short-term project, leading a major new initiative, or helping an interim team of people come together to solve a problem at your favorite charity, the task of preparing and planning is essential.

The lack of adequate preparation represents one of the primary reasons for the demise of many projects. Without a clear path for moving your initiative forward, it will be more difficult to assemble a team of committed individuals to work with you. While you may be successful in getting their initial time commitment, you will be less likely to successfully garner their long-term commitment of time and talents. And personal commitment counts for much more than the amount of time you clock in each day. Also, when you are trying to persuade individuals to join your effort, most want to know:

1. *Why* are you doing this particular project or activity?
2. *What* needs to be accomplished?
3. *Where* will their energy and expertise be best applied?
4. *How* do you intend to proceed?
5. *When* is the initiative to be completed?

Without preparation and planning, answers to these questions will not provide the type of detail needed by those you are attempting to convince related to the *value* of the project. Furthermore, the "team" can help define all the Who? What? Where? When? Why? and How? of your initiative.

Finally, preparation and planning provide the framework needed for managing your team's efforts. Without it, there is a strong likelihood that people will go off in several different directions, leading to the demise of your project. Needless to say, the confidence in your ability as a leader to organize and successfully manage projects will also be eroded. The result is that confidence, *in itself, is essential for you to remain a leader, as well as serving as a critical resource for team members.* And that confidence is held emblematically by you as the leader. So, I urge you to prepare and plan...

Champions keep playing until they get it right.

Billie Jean King
one of the most winningest
tennis pros in the history of the sport

Adopt a Learning Systems Approach in Your Work – Confidence is enhanced if continuous learning is held as a value for your projects or initiatives. The notion of *continuous quality improvement* (CQI) is increasingly recognized as a method for driving value in enterprises as far afield as manufacturing cars, software development, ensuring the right outcomes in the surgical suite at your local hospital, and any number of other examples from across all industries. However, it is more than simply improving the quality of a specific project, product, or process. It is also about sharing the knowledge and incorporating the learnings derived from copious project oversight to provide a detailed roadmap for training the next team to perform the same functions quicker, better, and faster.

In the healthcare field, for example, many large organizations have adopted a model for supporting the adoption of knowledge as "learning health systems." Such organizations pay particular attention to capturing information on the process of how work is done, examining the work processes in detail with the support of a diverse team rather than just a singular professional perspective, and openly sharing findings for all to review and consider, with methods for gaining the feedback of everyone. Such an approach has been shown to dramatically increase the rapidity of successful change adoption with improved outcomes and results. This approach can be readily adopted for other industries as well.

But it's not just knowledge. It is also the training and, in some cases, re-education that are required within an organization to increase confidence in changing processes, which will contribute to better outcomes. Training is at the heart of successful organizations. They not only learn but also apply their knowledge by giving back to others in the form of skill set modification or enhancement. This is an area that demands further attention from leaders at all different levels within your initiative if you are going to be successful in helping your company through successful transformations.

Be Openly Assertive Without Arrogance – If you can manage criticism, understand your strengths and weaknesses, have prepared and planned appropriately, and have adopted a learning systems approach, you hold the requisite tools for being openly assertive. So, what's the difference between being "assertive" and "openly assertive"? I don't mean to split hairs, but the difference is crucial. When you are "assertive," you present ideas with a closed perspective. You have the answer! When you are "openly assertive," you take the position that you know what you are doing for what reasons and how. But, by being "open," you consider and evaluate better ideas, approaches, or methods as well as the adoption of more contemporary knowledge or learning that may change your assertions. Given the data and results, as well as the potential implications of new data or information, it is clear that you are willing to modify or adjust your course of action. In other words, you need to put aside any dogmatic or blind thinking in "your" approach toward solving a problem.

Such an approach in the pursuit of persistence is an admirable quality and one that your followers will find worthy of support. It will increase their confidence in your leadership. Adopting these strategies will greatly enhance your sense of inner confidence, as well as your outer confidence among those around you. Together, these two parallel characteristics will not only bring you sustainable outcomes but also increased support from the team around you. Enough said, go make it work!

Enhancing Focus Through Tenacity – One of the most important contributions you can make to your persistence portfolio is the ability to focus.[23] In our daily lives, there are an increasing number of distractions that make it quite difficult to be productive. The literature is replete with examples of how the lack of distraction recognition in our lives serves as a major impediment toward actually completing tasks or moving the object of our attention forward. Some of these distractions are apparent. For example, the cacophony we experience from television, the lost time on social media, the many, many texts and emails that seemingly assault us all, as well as the constant distractions by alarms and whistles emanating from your "smart device," are examples that pull all of us away from what is directly in front of us. How many times have you experienced a situation where you're involved in a discussion on some detail when the interference of technology intrudes and derails the conversation? While the devices can contribute to efficiency, they can also contribute to inefficiency if not properly managed.

These distractions can foster bad habits if we allow them to take over our lives. Bad habits are perhaps the number one cause of loss of productivity. They lead to procrastination, worry, and anxiety by simply creating negative energy in our lives. Furthermore, these bad habits often become internalized when they become an addiction from the release of internal chemicals that stimulate our neurological alert functions excessively and cause a definitive loss of focus and productivity.

Focus is a five-letter word like no other, having a significant impact on our lives. When we offer our full focus on a single task, we often perform much better than when we multitask. Consider the number of traffic accidents now known to be directly caused by device distractions. Driving requires focus. Humans are not computers that can simultaneously process information on web browsers when we are trying to focus on other important tasks. We are, after all, human. We can't keep track of multiple tabs and expect to excel on every single one simultaneously. Nada – it does not work!

Zen Buddhism espouses the quality of being focused on a single task, to have a mind that does not waver from it. If you are working and only focusing on your work, you will find that the quality of work you produce will be better. If you are loving, only focus on love, and you will find that your love will be stronger in the long run. The greatest athletes and artists hold high levels of focus in their areas of expertise. Nikola Tesla was focused on the science of electricity and magnetism. Michael Jordan had no other focus except for basketball during his time with the Chicago Bulls basketball team. Picasso's focus was on art. Mozart's focus was on music. Get lost in your passion, and you will achieve true focus. Often, when we are focused on something we are passionate about, we lose track of time. "Is it already tomorrow?" will often pop up as a curious thought.

Focus and persistence are part of the same dynamic. One of the biggest challenges for individuals engaged in a recurring task that requires persistence is maintaining focus on the task at hand. As an example, many people have New Year's resolutions, but it would be interesting to see how many of those resolutions persist for more than just a few weeks.

In addition to our focus on the moment, there is also a need to focus on the trajectory.[24] If we don't maintain our sense of direction, we can end up letting the moments dictate our endpoint. As a result – and I know this is repetitive – we need to have clarity on our goals. At any given moment during the day, there are no doubt multiple initiatives or projects demanding our attention and focus. By allowing ourselves to become distracted by the multiplicity of opportunities we are likely misplacing our energy and effort on the work that we do not need to do...that will not help us accomplish our overall objective...that does not help us move from where we are to where we've planned to be...and, therefore, the need for focus...

Why does this happen? Is it the need to be needed? Is the increasingly distracted world we live in, on a minute-to-minute basis, where incoming emails, texts, phone calls, and the like bombard us with distractions, diminishing – if not destroying – our ability to focus? Some have surmised that we are increasingly being asked to deal with minor queries and intrusions by offering us the opportunity to "solve an isolated problem" rather than deal with the weightier problems that come with accepting a leadership role.

While all of these can be reasons for diminishing our ability to focus, a willingness to accept results rather than the right results is a key reason. We often get caught up in the moment when, in fact, we should focus on the long-term consequences and the downstream effects of our actions. By allowing the moment to captivate our focus and direction, we give up the opportunity to set a clear direction either for ourselves or for the organizations we lead. Based on my experience, maintaining focus is one of the most demanding tasks for any leader.

Sustained effort over time is the key to focus. The metaphor that comes to mind is sailing. I once had the opportunity to join a weekend group of occasional sailors who sailed fairly regularly, which means we needed "all" of the talent in the group to sail our boat. When allowed to steer the ship, I learned that it was not a simple task of setting the direction and joining the group in conversation. No!! Indeed, it required constant attention and reorientation so that our destination remained the target. Without such focus, it was very easy to drift in all sorts of directions as we were cast about by the action of waves, conversation, other sailors enjoying the bay, and any number of other distractions. Maintaining a focus on the task at hand became a clear and essential function when serving as the helmsman of the ship, or the task of the person steering the vessel. Serving as the leader of an organization is very much the same type of task. Maintaining focus and direction is crucial...and often results in the following:

- Although it takes more energy and effort to maintain focus, the result is far better...
- You might arrive at the destination of your choice...
- The people around you will have greater clarity on what their respective areas of focus should be...

- Resources will not be needlessly wasted in the pursuit of misaligned activities...
- Your organization does not run aground with you in the helmsman position...

The organization will benefit from a consistent focus, as will the individuals serving it, who are likely expending their time, energy, and devotion on the mission. Another benefit of sustained focus is that the organization's values come to life. The team's actions lead to demonstrable results, and the organization gains energy from the momentum the team generates. Such is the power of focus...

But, there is a need for more than focus. There is also a need for **tenacity,** for it has been said before: *Not all storms come to disrupt your life. Some come to clear your path.*[25] So, let's consider a metaphor...

The Sisyphus' Forever Story – In considering tenacity, we first need to consider the story of Sisyphus, the mythical Greek king cursed with the task of forever pushing a rock up a hill. Can you imagine? Especially, forever? In Greek mythology, Sisyphus was the son of King Aeolus of Thessaly and Queen Enarete. From that point forward in the story, the various connections among all the relatives become rather complex. For those interested in the interrelations and web of familial connections for Sisyphus, I refer you to the Wikipedia website for Greek mythology. The site will serve as a starter kit for anything and everything you ever wanted to know about Greek mythology.

Sisyphus founded and became the first King of Ephyra, also known as Corinth, in Greek mythology. Over time, the city became a commercial hub for the Islands due to the investments that Sisyphus made in navigation. The problem was that he was a sly, deceitful, and treacherous leader who regularly violated the Xenia, or code of hospitality and generosity that should always be shown to guests and travelers who fell upon one's shores. Instead, Sisyphus tended to kill them for various reasons, most of which were unjustified.

Zeus, the father of the gods in Greek mythology, did not approve of Sisyphus's actions. He became particularly infuriated when Sisyphus told the river god, Asopus, that his daughter, Aegina, had been kidnapped by Zeus. You can see that the story is getting rather complicated. When Asopus discovered the kidnapping, he created a spring flood on the Acropolis of Corinth that caused all sorts of damage.

It was at this point that Zeus decided that enough was enough. He asked Thanatos – the personification of death – to take Sisyphus and chain him up in the Underworld. To make it happen, Thanatos went to Sisyphus with the chains in hand and asked him how they worked. Being the wise and ruthless leader, Sisyphus quickly chained up Thanatos, with the result being that with Thanatos (death) chained up, no mortal could die and go to the Underworld. But the story doesn't stop there.

Ares, the god of war, became very aggravated with the situation because, with the lack of wars, no one was dying, and wars were no longer interesting. Through considerable surreptitious effort, Ares was able to release Thanatos from his chains and at the same time, trap Sisyphus, who was then handed over to Thanatos. The story continues with many ups and downs in the life of Sisyphus, where he essentially angered many of his fellow gods and goddesses. In the end, Zeus finally had enough of the cunning and hubris of Sisyphus and punished him by giving him the task of eternally pushing a boulder uphill, which was chained to him. The problem for Sisyphus was that as soon as he reached the top of the hill, the boulder would roll off his shoulder and fall back down the hill, pulling Sisyphus with him, thereby requiring yet another effort at pushing the boulder up the hill. Such is the task of tenacity at times...

Considering Tenacity Today – If we move beyond Greek mythology, there are many Sisyphean stories we could point to in the lives of leaders. How many times have you felt like you were almost there when everything seemed to fall apart? Some of the most compelling examples of tenacity emanate from injuries that people experience in times of war or trauma.[26] Marcus Kuboy entered the Army as a young man in 2005 to train as a medic. He says, "I didn't want to go in there and shift the scales of the war one way or the other. But I just wanted to help out where I could. Be effective. I take a lot of pride in the country, and there are kids going over there and getting hurt, and there was a part of me that wanted to go in there and help them."

While on patrol near Fallujah, Kuboy's convoy was hit by a roadside bomb. He barely lived through the incident. His legs were badly injured, along with his feet, which were shattered. He sustained a broken jaw and was left unconscious with moderate brain injury. He describes the incident with some humor by noting, "I was pretty intelligent before I got the brain injury, and that intelligence is still present, but my processing speed has been slowed down." It is only through his daily, tenacious effort that Marcus has been able to resume a more normal life. He now serves as an advocate for the Minnesota Brain Injury Alliance, helping to inform others about the services and programs available to people in his state or those with similar injuries. He's moved from medic to spokesman – with a cause. Sometimes we end up taking on roles and positions that we had no intention of filling at the beginning of our life's journey. Such is the path of leaders...

Fast Company, in 2013, defined five characteristics of an effective leader.[27] Number 3 on the list was a "group" of characteristics lumped together as: "...courage, tenacity, and patience. Having the courage to stand alone, the tenacity to not succumb to pressure, and the patience to keep fighting until you win the day–and sometimes being able to do all three at the same time." The combination of these three is not necessarily a "success cocktail" but more a combination of skills that you will need to bring together, develop and nurture to be a true and successful leader.

In some respects, tenacity is the process of continuously scanning your environment, absorbing new information or data, making adjustments, setting new directions, or defining new pathways for solving the problems you face. Too frequently, leaders fall into the trap of looking for quick leadership development solutions or workshops. In other words:

- What is the magic pill I can take to make myself a better leader?
- What is the most effective approach I can take to help my team work more effectively together?

While these can be helpful if taken in the right dose, tenacity will yield results over the long term. It is a *process,* not a *solution,* for serving as an effective leader! For those who have worked in more entrepreneurial situations, tenacity is not just a virtue but a requirement. My former boss, Ross Perot Sr., whom I admire greatly, once said, "No doesn't mean no—just *not now*." And that means – keep working on it! Furthermore, in his support of the tenacious spirit, he always held forth those leaders who would work on solving a problem even when it meant consuming more resources than originally planned, if the result of the effort was a solution to a problem for the customer. Tenaciousness was held forth as a "North Star," which is true for many entrepreneurial companies.

The tenacious spirit is part of the essential foundation for the House of Persistence! As part of the House of Persistence, tenacity enables leaders to build a solid foundation based on the four cornerstones of Purpose, Commitment, Confidence, and Focus, thereby creating and supporting a successful team, program, company, or even a nation through **persistence**. Like the earlier discussion about "inherent nudging", tenacity is more than simply trying harder.

The first cornerstone in the House of Persistence is **purpose,** which requires an essential belief in oneself to carry you forward in the face of discomfort, doubt, dissuasion, or delay, which are part and parcel of any major initiative. What I'm trying to convey is the important point that a leader needs to let their *purpose* shine through. When your team and the people you work with understand what your drivers are, where you are headed, and why, they are much more likely to get on board and help make your vision a reality.

The second cornerstone in the House of Persistence is **commitment**. It is exemplified in how we do our work as leaders. Are we consistent? Do we let the object of our desires or our intent stand above any personal motivations?

For example, my commitment for many, many years has been to "make health care better." It's been a consistent part of the jobs I've assumed. It's the part of my professional life that I hold forth above other considerations. It may have even gotten in the way of my personal life at times, which is always a constant area to monitor as a leader. Lessons learned: commitments are important, but we need to balance those commitments against the impact they can have on family, friends, teammates, and others with whom we are closely aligned.

The third cornerstone in the House of Persistence is *confidence*, which may be the hardest of the four to maintain. When we go down the wrong path, when we mismanage our resources, when we face failure – those are times when the erosion of confidence can be very high. Yet, if we accept these failures and learn from them, they can also be incredible resources for rebuilding our confidence and making our organizations even stronger. Accomplishing such a feat requires internal sustenance as well as external affirmation. Taking care of yourself, eating properly, getting sufficient sleep, maintaining perspective, and keeping the other elements of persistence clearly in view are crucial ingredients for maintaining one's capacity as a leader and rebuilding confidence.

Finally, the fourth cornerstone in the House of Persistence is the *focus*. When we can persistently focus on the problems at hand, we can learn and more readily work to improve our initiative. Then, and only then, can the leader become the master of their world. Most problems are not resolved quickly. Rather, they require consistent and continuous effort over time. Tenacity with your vision, your goals, and your expected outcomes are critical expectations that you must hold high among those you work with if your selected path of persistence is to realize results.

CHAPTER VII

On Vulnerability

It's not the critic who counts; not the man who points out how the strong man stumbles or where the doer of deeds could have done them better. The credit belongs to the man who is actually in the arena, whose face is marred by dust and sweat and blood; who strives valiantly... who at best knows the triumph of high achievement and who at the worst, if he fails, at least fails while daring greatly.

Theodore Roosevelt
26th President of the United States
In comments made in his famous *"Man in the Arena,"*
a speech delivered at the Sorbonne
on April 23, 1910, in Paris, France

In shifting our focus to vulnerability, we come face-to-face with the hardest element on the path of persistence for leaders. Aside from outright failure, it's probably the hardest element to incorporate into our persistence armamentarium.

Comparisons in Vulnerability — I suspect that most people have only rarely seen a leader openly acknowledge their vulnerability on an issue or problem.

These moments are rare, but when they do occur, they are incredibly powerful. Witness the difference in the response of President Barack Obama and President Donald Trump to comparable issues:

President Barack Obama[28] – On December 14, 2012, in the quiet community of Newtown, Connecticut, Adam Lanza entered Sandy Hook Elementary School. He fatally shot 20 children between the ages of six and seven, as well as six adult staff members. He had killed his mother at home before driving to Sandy Hook. When the first responders arrived at the school, Lanza committed suicide. The incident shocked the nation as the deadliest mass shooting at a school in US history and among the deadliest of all mass shootings across all places. It was in the aftermath of the Newtown tragedy that President Barack Obama was brought to tears twice during his address to the nation, where he expressed his "overwhelming grief" on behalf of the nation. He continued by dabbing at his eyes and stating,

> *"Each time I learn the news, I react not as a president, but as anyone else would — as a parent. And that was especially true today...The majority of those who died today were children – beautiful little kids between the ages of five and ten years old [Followed by a 12-second pause where he wiped his eyes a couple of times]. They had their entire lives ahead of them — birthdays, graduations, weddings, kids of their own [Followed by a second 6-second pause and more wiping of the eyes]."* He continued by stating, *"Among the fallen were also teachers, men, and women who devoted their lives to helping children fulfill their dreams."*

In that moment of quiet wiping away of the tears, President Obama exhibited a vulnerability that brought the nation together in our national grief over what had occurred to innocent children and their teachers. He brought the nation together.

President Donald Trump[29] – In an eerily similar incident, Mr. Trump faced a similar mass shooting at Marjory Stoneman Douglas High School in Parkland, Florida, on February 14, 2018. Seventeen people were killed and seventeen more were wounded – all with an AR-15 semi-automatic rifle – making it one of the deadliest school massacres in history across the entire world. The perpetrator, 19-year-old Nikolas Jacob Cruz, confessed shortly after his arrest. In addressing the nation, President Trump said,

> *"To every parent, teacher, and child who is hurting so badly, we are here for you for whatever you need, whatever we can do to ease your pain. No child, no teacher should ever be in danger in an American school... We are committed to working with state and local leaders to serve our schools and tackle the difficult issue of mental health."*

Throughout the entire statement, the President looks to his left and the front center – obviously to a teleprompter – and reads from the script without emotion or feeling. There was no vulnerability.

The difference between the two statements to the nation was and is palpable. As a nation, we like to think of the President of the United States as a "leader of leaders." In one instance, the clear sense of feeling pushes through the veneer of technology and reaches out to the listener with true compassion. In the other instance, the lack of emotion is equally evident – like reading a script minus the emotion of the actor. Both announcements are available on YouTube, and it is worth watching both to gain a better sense of how vulnerability is conveyed – or, rather, isn't.

Another example is of the Dalai Lama from a 2011 video in Hunsur, India, where he spoke about his past and *bodhicitta*[30], a Buddhist concept meaning the "mind of enlightenment" that cultivates compassion. The video went viral on YouTube. As one of the most beloved spiritual leaders in the world, the Dalai Lama started the presentation by outlining the importance of bodhicitta as an approach that all of us should cultivate to reach the "altruistic mind cherishing others over oneself." It was at this point that he broke down sobbing before his disciples as they waited in silence for him to continue. In this moment of vulnerability, he revealed to the entire planet the very power and strength of his *bodhicitta* and empathy for others.

Brene Brown[31] has described vulnerability as "...our most accurate measure of courage." She notes quite aptly that revealing our vulnerabilities is one of the first things that others look for during their initial interactions with us, but it is one of the very last things we are willing to share with others. The contradictions are stark. Why is that the case?

The overwhelming tone of leadership tomes over the centuries does not offer an expression of vulnerability as a core characteristic of leadership. As an example, Machiavelli in his book, *The Prince*, notes:

> *"A question arises: whether it be better to be loved than feared or feared than loved? It may be answered that one should wish to be both, but because it is difficult to unite them in one person, it is much safer to be feared than loved, when, of the two, either must be dispensed with."*

In essence, Machiavelli argues that we must understand our tolerance for vulnerability in the presence of others if we want to be a trusted leader. And, by stating that it is "safer to be feared than loved," Machiavelli goes further by defining the very essence of the presence of authoritarian leaders throughout history. The foundation of fear is established through intimidation, control, and the management of situations that arise, all of which are kept under control to lessen their vulnerability. But, although it may be an easier mode for controlling an environment, an organization, or a country, in the broader construct, it is far less effective for engaging those with whom we work. Control is simple. Sharing our vulnerabilities in the open is engaging and allows us to be embraced.

I am not suggesting you lay all your innermost vulnerabilities on the table. Rather, consider allowing those around you to know that you do not have all the answers, that you are open to input, and that you desire their perspective. Such are the elements of useful vulnerability that will ultimately engage those with whom you are working to mobilize for the goals you set forth. And, through such an approach, your persistence will shine through. Furthermore, by integrating the answers, input, and perspectives of those with whom you are working to assist you, they will become part of your mission by supporting and fostering your persistence.

Finally, vulnerability cannot be contrived. It must be real...and consistent. With such an approach, your abilities and strength as a leader are enhanced beyond all you could do by yourself through other means. Consider it!

The Crucial Task

Assess

Successes And Faiures

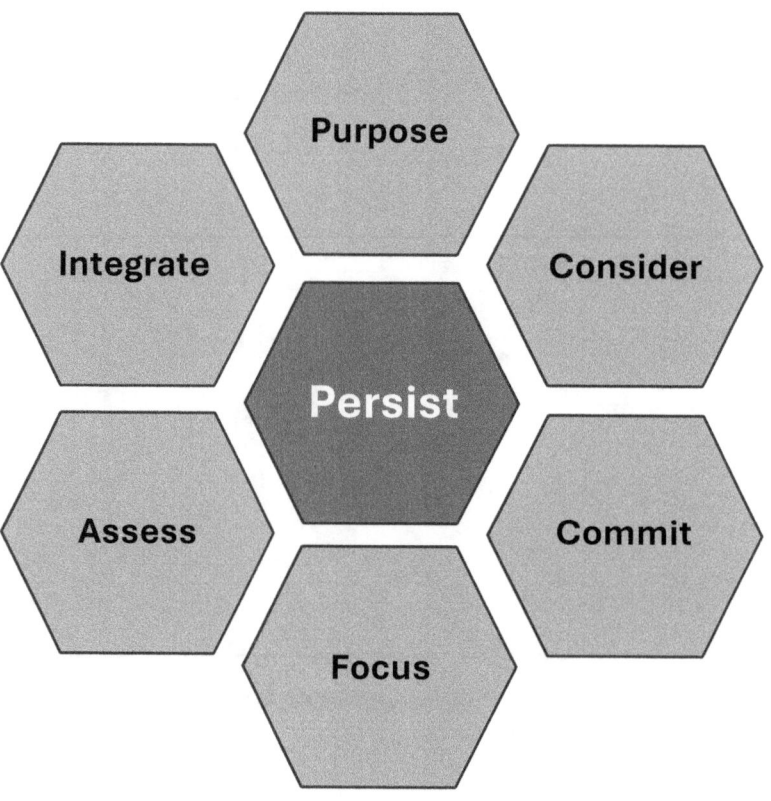

CHAPTER VIII

Learning From Failure

Failure should be our teacher, not our undertaker.
Failure is delay, not defeat.
It is a temporary detour, not a dead end.
Failure is something we can avoid by saying nothing, doing
nothing, being nothing.

Denis Waitley
Author, The Psychology of Winning

On Failure — Sometimes a song is the best way to describe what happens in life. So, it was for Marion Montgomery, a jazz singer born in Natchez, Mississippi. She began her career in Atlanta, working at local clubs where she was discovered by Peggy Lee. In 1963, she recorded a wonderful song released by Capital Records that went nowhere. It was written by Dean Kay and Kelly Gordon under the auspicious title of "*That's Life,*" but it failed to chart. Failing to chart meant that the song was going nowhere fast, since few artists would be willing to consider it for a recording.

The song was also recorded by another jazz singer, O.C. Smith. His rendition went in the same direction as Ms. Montgomery's, and it did not even come close to making the Billboard 100. However, O.C.'s version caught the ear of a star who had risen to the farthest heights of the music business and fallen like so many others.

However, when he decided to record the song, he sang it with his emphasis and vocal energy in a non-jazz, popular-based format. Within months, his version topped the Billboard 100 as a #4 hit and, on the Easy Listening chart, reached #1 for three weeks straight in December 1966. It's a song that teaches us how to cope with the ups and downs of failure. "*That's Life*" goes like this...

> *That's life...that's what all the people say*
> *You're ridin' high in April, shot down in May*
> *But I know I'm gonna change that tune*
> *When I'm back on top, back on top in June...*

And, from there, the tune weaves a story of the ups and downs of being a puppet, a pauper, a pirate, a poet – and, on to a king, because "that's life."

For those with some recollection of the '60s and '70s, you probably recognize the song sung by Frank Sinatra in the fall of 1966. He was working on a new album at Western Recorders with his producer when he was introduced to the song "*That's Life.*" He loved the song and recorded it with an orchestra conducted by Donnie Lanier. Before this point, Sinatra had met with some degree of success but was generally confined to working in Las Vegas as part of the Rat Pack. He had made countless recordings, but none of them had gone anywhere for nearly 10 years until "*That's Life*" was released. Within four weeks of release, his rendition moved to the top of the charts. Many observers consider it the anthem of resilience, a celebration of strength, and a voice of determination for overcoming life's challenges and failures.

When you start to research persistence, the most common concept mentioned is *failure,* which is defined in the dictionary as: 1) the lack of success or, 2) the omission of expected or required action. If there is an area of persistence that is one of the most underappreciated in our contemporary culture, it is failure. It seems to me that the most important lesson in the whole discussion of failure is the recognition that *to embrace persistence one must first accept the possibility of failure, for failure gives purpose to persistence.*

Yes, indeed! Failure does give purpose to persistence! And yet, failure is not so simplistic as one singular word. It encompasses many different characteristics associated with failure. Certain aspects focus on the failure of "hard" elements, such as devices, equipment, or items. Other aspects to consider include soft elements, such as systems or processes. Many diverse causes and mechanisms can result in the evolution of failures and the inevitable consequences derived from those failures.[32]

Yet, despite the clear advantages of understanding why a failure has occurred, most individuals and organizations simply do not incorporate, nor do they effectively integrate, the lessons derived and learned from an understanding of their failure. According to a paper in the *Harvard Business Review* on "Strategies for Learning from Failure,"[33] many diverse organizations have attempted to develop programs for learning from failure. In medicine, we have postmortem exams and Grand Rounds. At NASA, the space shuttle program conducts design reviews. Within the aviation industry, Service Difficulty Reports (SDRs) are submitted for every incident that occurs, with the reports distributed to the manufacturer, the Federal Aviation Administration, and NASA officials. The result is that failure analysis can range from simple and voluntary activities to very complex regulatory requirements.

The other key element in failure is that most leaders and executives of organizations view failure solely in the negative context as "wrong," "mistaken," or "deficient," where "blame," "attribution," and "causation" can be applied to the people or processes in the organization. The result is that failure recognition is not desired by most organizations, except in Silicon Valley, where the mantra "fail early, fail fast" has been adopted by many start-ups and ongoing technology companies. The philosophy is based on the recognition that failure is endemic in the venture-backed world; therefore, the earlier a failure is recognized and resolved, the better. The only problem with this approach is that it again embraces the negative. On the positive side, while failure can result in a loss of funding, an effective team can learn, respond, and mitigate quickly to resolve the problem(s).

Let me be clear: Failure can be bad, but not always. Organizations or individuals that embrace failure as a process of *learning* can accelerate their capabilities. Attention to the details of *why* failures occur, *how* the problem can be alleviated, and what is within the team's power to change can be a powerful model for fostering the creative resolution of problems. Furthermore, the range of lessons learned can extend from the fact that procedures were not followed, to the identification of an abrasive behavior by a member of the team, to a recognition that the market was not ready for a product, all of which impinge upon the ultimate capability of the organization to resolve problems and move forward. As I noted at the outset: *To embrace persistence one must first accept the possibility of failure, for failure gives purpose to persistence.* As we will learn in the next chapter, we must "learn" from our experiences to gain value from failure.

All of this means that we must reconsider our notions of success and carefully examine *what* we can do to proactively prevent failure while simultaneously embracing the *why* and *how* of failure. As we consider these ideas, it is important to remind everyone that learning from failure, while important, is not the end-all and be-all of persistence. It is a part of persistence. And, while the prior concepts like purpose, commitment, confidence, and focus highlighted in the prior chapters are crucial, it is simultaneously and equally important, if not more so, to fully understand failure.

To facilitate effective adoption of the important lessons derived from failure, there are some key ideas you must incorporate into your failure analysis. Here are a few thoughts:

1. **Pursue Your Purpose** – Many of us carry around business cards. I've always carried two types. Why? Because I have worked for various businesses that held their brand, style, and image, which they wanted to create, foster, and convey. In many respects, your purpose is your brand.

When people see your brand, they should be reminded of your purpose. As one of the leaders in the organization, I needed to be a part of the team to help carry those points forward. At the same time, I am an individual. I have my brand, style, and image, which is the essence of me. So, I had personal cards made as well. Those cards are meant for friends, acquaintances, and personal colleagues. It's who I am. Let me digress for a moment to make the point.

A second element of my brand is that I always wear a whisk on my left lapel of whatever I happen to be wearing! The most frequent question I get on almost a daily basis is: "Is that a whisk/whip/stirrer on your lapel?" And, my response: "Yes, I think I'm a good cook." Then, after a brief pause, I add: "And, I really like to stir things up!" My wife – if she is with me – usually replies, "No, he actually just stirs up trouble!" As you can see, the whisk has become an integral part of my brand, style, and image, to the extent that it is featured as the emblem on my business card, bringing us full circle.

The tagline on my business card reads: "*...inspiring creative change to benefit the human condition.*" It is my purpose...extended. As I've considered various jobs and become involved in different volunteer activities, I strive to collaborate with others and my community to improve people's lives. In essence, when I *stir things up*, lurking in the background is my commitment to this statement of purpose. I continue to wear the whisk daily on whatever I wear that day. It has become my new branding moniker.

So, the questions are:

- Have you written your purpose down?
- Do you know why you do what you do?
- Are you clear with the world on why and what you are doing as part of your personal and professional commitments?
- How is your purpose tied to you as an individual?

- Have you branded your purpose to yourself?
- Have you taken a conscious look at the failures in your life?
- What lessons have you learned?

If these questions are not part of your regular armamentarium of self-reflection, you are at risk of having more, rather than fewer, problems with failure...

2. **Adapt to the World** – The perspective of "adapting" is an important consideration for those who have worked/lived or want to work/live in different places or organizations. Why? In a word – culture. There are lots of definitions of culture that range in application from biology to anthropology. The definition that applies to this discussion is: *the sum total of ways of living built up by a group of human beings and transmitted from one generation to another.* Whether we are talking about corporations, collectives, or associations, the concept of culture is highly applicable. When the "way of living" gets "transmitted from one generation to another" repetitively, it generally gets stronger and stronger. I could point out many examples. If you look around any industry, you will find clear examples of a strong culture.

In fact, as part of my discussions with organizations when I start to work with them, the very first question I ask is: "Tell me about the culture of the organization." I've learned over time that if the culture does not fit me, my style, or approach toward solving problems, the organization will not allow me to fit its style or approach to solving problems. What this means for you as a leader is that you need to invest time to understand your personal emotional intelligence quotient. Ultimately, the world will not generally change quickly to accommodate a single individual.

There's another element in this equation as well. The blame game is too often used by people as an excuse for why they are not successful. How you react to and manage the events of your life is one of the most important factors in determining who you are in the world. So, if you are going to embark upon changing the culture of an organization, a group, a corporation, or a society – it will be important to change yourself first. You will need to fully understand the why and what of the change you are offering and, most importantly, you will need reinforcements. Isolated battles generally end in your demise (notice, I did not say "failure"). Reinforcements, soldiers of support, disciples – whatever you want to call them – are essential. Start there first...which means *adapting to the world so you can change it.*

3. **Manage the Details** – One of the best books I've read that highlights the importance of detail in preventing failure is *The River of Doubt* by Candice Millard.[34] It is an account of Theodore Roosevelt's final expedition to an uncharted river tributary in the Amazon Basin. As the 26th President of the United States at the turn of the last century, he was an amazing figure. Roosevelt had at his beck and call all the necessary resources to organize any type of expedition.

    As she recounts in her book, however, there were countless errors made by various individuals who held responsibility for the project. They ranged from the person responsible for selecting the type of boats to be used for traversing the Amazon's waters to the individual responsible for selecting food and supplies for the long trip through the wilderness. As an example, very late in the expedition, when they were about to begin their travels into an uncharted area, they decided that the volume of supplies needed to be whittled down to accommodate the smaller, less steady boats they had assembled. When they opened the crates containing the supplies, they "...discovered whole cases of olive oil, cases of mustard, malted milk, stuffed olives, prunes, applesauce, etc., etc., Even Rhine wine."[35] While these are important for the gourmand, to support survival, they can be put aside.

    A lesson that many leaders learn over time is that you can have all of the vision in the world, but you must also have all the help you can muster from those around you who manage the details.

4. **Love What You Do** — Another important lesson is to love what you do. This idea does not need a lot of expansive description. It's clear. So, do it! If you love what you do, your persistence quotient will allow you to meet all manner of obstacles, create boundless energy among your colleagues and co-workers, and meet failure with an openness for truly understanding the *why* and *what* needs to be done so that failure does not occur again.

5. **Embrace Your Failures** — Laurence Weinzimmer, Ph.D., a management professor at Bradley University, conducted a study several years ago in which he reviewed the content and recommendations of top leadership books marketed by various publishers. He noted:

   "They all basically said the same thing... They want you to believe the sky is always blue and the road is always smooth, but the sky is not always blue and the road is not always smooth. What we found with most of our interviews was that most leaders told us the most important lessons came from their toughest challenges, not from imitating somebody else's success."

   In *The Wisdom of Failure*,[36] Weinzimmer explores more fully the elements of failure. The book is worth a full read. However, the essence of his leadership lessons that must be followed includes:

   a. Know when to quit.
   b. Do not become sidetracked by the desire to make a quick profit.
   c. Do not define your efforts by comparison to other businesses.
   d. Do not try to be everything at once.
   e. Learn to delegate.

In essence, failure is an integral part of the persistence process. It is in failure that we ultimately gain. The literature is replete with examples of how learning from failure is valuable.[37] Yet, while many organizations embrace their failures by sharing them internally, discussing and debating, and planning responses to failures, it is the exception rather than the rule for organizations to actually *learn* from their failures. This holds true across all industries – from telecommunications and finance to consumer goods, pharmaceuticals, medical devices, hospitals, and healthcare clinics. Even organizations as deeply steeped in failure redesign, such as aviation and aeronautics, have difficulty "learning" from failure. Why? To a large extent, it's because the leaders of most organizations align failure with "bad outcomes."

And, Don't Forget To

...Integrate...

The Lessons Learned

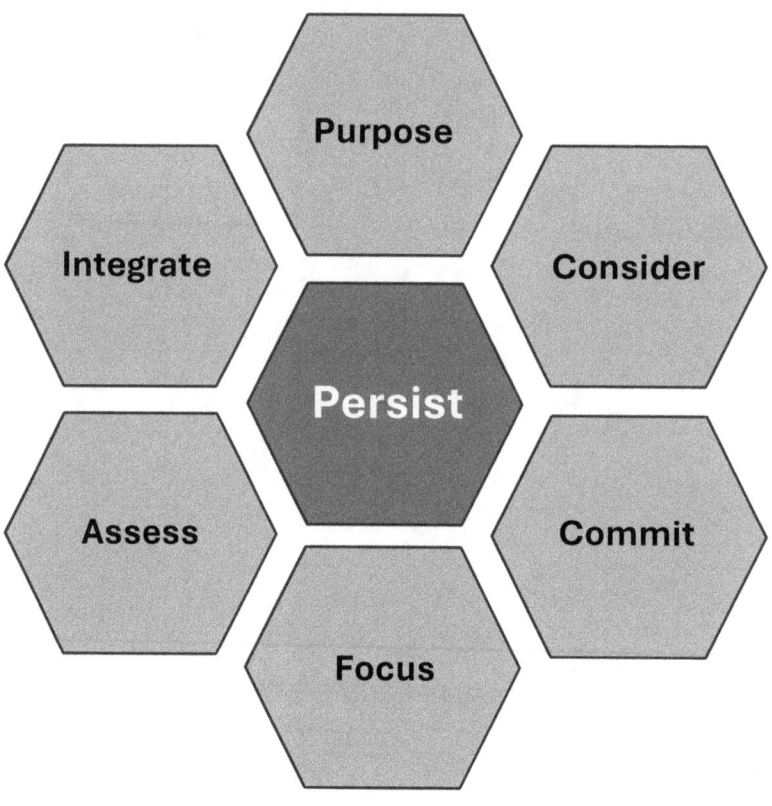

CHAPTER IX

Learning through Integration...

"Our method was to develop integrated products, and that meant our process had to be integrated and collaborative."

Steve Jobs

Founder & CEO of Apple on the underlying corporate philosophy used in developing the company

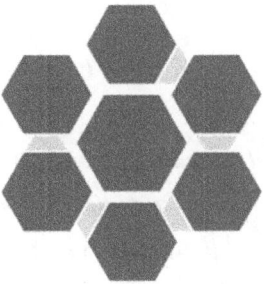

First, A Story – As we consider the issue of *learning*, it reminds me of a story often told of the Donkey and the Well. It's a great children's story filled with lessons on learning. And, like most children's stories, it starts with: *Once upon a time...*

...there was a donkey – an old donkey that was getting older, or as they say out in the hinterlands, "long in the tooth". The donkey was stupid, even stubborn. The farmer who owned the donkey had named him Kalytero shortly after he was born, which means "best" in Greek. But, over the years, the farmer came to loathe his donkey because of its stupidity and stubbornness, which made it very difficult to work with. He had become so annoyed with the donkey that in the last couple of years, he had renamed

the donkey Chazos, which means "stupid" in Greek. So, this simple donkey had gone from best to stupid, and the farmer treated him this way.

The farmer owned a rather large property, and one day, when he was out in the fields, he heard off in the distance a rather loud, distinctive "ey-ore, ey-ore" sound of a donkey. Now, the farmer didn't have any other donkeys, and he knew that none of the other farmers in the area had any either, so, he figured that the sound must be coming from Chazos. As he walked towards the sound, he shook his head back and forth, wondering what the stupid donkey had done now. It was then that he came upon an old abandoned well near the corner of one of his fields. To his dismay, as he looked down into the well, he immediately saw that Chazos was at the bottom, trapped and unable to climb out.

Well, the farmer was exasperated, and he'd had enough. Shouting out to the empty fields around him, he yelled, "That's it! I'm done." The farmer pulled out his phone and rang up his neighbors, asking each of them to bring a shovel. Since the donkey's stupidity was well known throughout the countryside, they all agreed that this was an opportunity to get rid of the donkey by burying him in the old, dried-up well.

All of the farmer's friends came over, and they started working together to shovel dirt into the well. At first, the donkey brayed loudly and protested loudly, but after about 10 minutes, the braying stopped. And the farmers kept shoveling. After another 10 minutes, one of the farmers said to the group, "Hey, let's take a look. Maybe we can stop shoveling." So, they all walked over to the old dry well and looked inside. To their astonishment, the donkey was simply standing on the large mound of dirt they had thrown in the well, staring back at them quietly and breathing ever so slowly.

It was at this point that the farmers realized they needed to change their approach; instead of burying the donkey, they should try to save him. So, they redoubled their efforts by shoveling more and more dirt into the old, dried, abandoned well until the donkey was able to jump out of the well to gain his release. When Chazos jumped out, the farmers all dropped their shovels and applauded and cheered with a newfound admiration for this stupid, stubborn donkey. They were so taken by the way the donkey had solved the problem by climbing up on the piles of dirt they had thrown in the well that they rechristened him as Kalyteros or "best."

There are many times in life when we feel "stupid," like Chazos, the donkey. But we are not stupid. Just as dirt has been thrown into the well of our lives, it is often thrown on our backs. However, if we learn from it and utilize the information, ideas, energy, and other elements that are often overlooked in failures, we are no longer trapped. Rather, we can build on those experiences by learning from them. And, through those learnings, we are no longer trapped or buried. We can stand on our experiences and find a way to solve the problems we face. It's the challenge we must face with persistence.

Fostering Failure Adoption Through Active Integration – The art of *integration* is one of the most important elements of persistence. Suppose we fail to actively integrate the learnings, including both the apparent and the hidden ones, derived from our experiences of trying to facilitate change. In that case, we are likely to fail again or at least be markedly delayed in achieving our objectives because of blindness to underlying problems with our persistent objective. When organizations or initiatives actively review their failings, asking...

Who else should have been at the table helping us?

What could have been done differently?

Where should we have intervened?

How did we miss those problems?

Why did we get the results we did?

...They get a better understanding!! There's also another set of *Who? What? Where? Why?* questions associated with deeper learning, so keep on reading; those issues will be addressed shortly.

In essence, to truly solve problems, we must intentionally engage in what is described as "activated learning." Perhaps the best way to initiate active learning and avoid failure is to consider the Kolb A[4] Learning Cycle[38] or, *First Assess, Then Assemble, Apply, and Activate*. It provides a straightforward approach to how learning occurs. In the model,

- **Assess** the situation by gathering information and knowledge that can be used to frame the problems. The assessment phase should, as a matter of practice, become an integral activity for any successful organization as part of the natural evolution of work that emanates from a failure of any type. If practiced as part of an ongoing approach to problem-solving, the results of the assessment can evolve from a simple collection of information fragments to the gradual accumulation of information that supports a true understanding. Such understanding is often preceded or precipitated by an "aha" experience of knowledge. Either way, it is an important first step in the cycle of change.

- **Assemble** the right people and resources for implementing a revised process or workflow. The work of assembling will change behaviors by creating new approaches to work in the organization, engaging customers or others with whom you work in more productive ways, and the list goes on, by considering the who, what, where, when, and how of the work. It is important to note that the process of "assembling" is not rigid. It also actively considers the internal culture and dynamics of the organization. The essence of continuous learning requires consideration of organizational culture and becomes a part of the fabric of how work is accomplished in the workplace setting at all times.

- ***Apply*** the newfound knowledge. If nothing is done with the knowledge, the value of going through the previous two tasks is for naught, and there is little worth in the effort for the organization. Without application, the problems identified by the team of individuals assembled to solve the problem will essentially have been a wasted effort. Therefore, applying the newfound knowledge by putting it into trial practice, trying out the proposed solutions, and seeing if they make a difference, while reassessing the results, is crucial.

- ***Activate***, the last phase, is perhaps the most difficult. Leaders must take action to activate the solution across the entire organization. At this point, the formal adoption of the new knowledge is integrated into the armamentarium of skills and capabilities by engaging in the work of the entire team. The activation stage is the moment of transformation. Resistance should be expected. Some will respond by sharing doubts about whether the change made a real difference. Such a response is the actual reason for the three previous steps and the need for documentation – to engage the naysayers as advocates for the change. It is a crucial step because it is where new knowledge and processes are integrated with pre-existing approaches to life in the organization. It becomes a new approach to how operations will work from that point forward.

The A^4 cycle has applications not only within organizations but also for all manner of problem-solving across a diverse array of problems in life. It provides the requisite rigor that supports leaders who embrace continuous learning as a model for creating a dynamic organization or work process. The use of A^4 is how effective leaders grow and continually refine their skills. Another example comes from an email I received in early 2017 from a colleague with whom I had worked over the years. Her comments were prescient on the topic of "learning." She sent this note after we had worked on a project that had come to nil. It captures the essence of how we need to consider the challenges that lie before us as leaders:

All the starts and stops - all the discoveries in your life are a steady bedrock to launch ideas from. At this point in time, I find that I return more and more to previous endeavors that were before their time - or even just ignored in the wrong setting. I have often combined seemingly failed ideas, finally finding a context for previous research, discovery, or theory. If you are early in your career, consider any "dead end" - simply a pause! Keep those notes, those renderings, the draft prototypes, and the methodology that fell on deaf ears warm and ready. The right moment or circumstance will eventually arrive, and you will recognize the opportunity more readily and be several steps ahead.[39]

Therefore, follow this advice:

1. Keep those notes.
2. Save the failed ideas.
3. Readjust your prototypes.
4. Accumulate learnings.

If you apply these suggestions, you will arrive at a moment when the timing is right, the circumstances are correct, and the opportunity is present for using your prior learnings to solve a new problem. It is the point where we, as leaders, reach the stage where the accumulation of information nuggets truly contributes immensely to advanced learning. Whether it's learning how to walk, learning how to do calculus, learning how to build better buildings by using newly evolved construction products, managing the approach toward customer engagement, or learning how to diagnose a skin disease, it is the accumulated knowledge that, when put together properly, reveals itself as learning.

The vast majority of learning we all experience over time is not simply a happenstance situation. It's not like lightning bolts hitting the ground. Rather, it is a product of persistence! Each experience we have as leaders adds to our prior learning portfolio. The question that often gets asked is: "But is there a way to infuse learning into our organizations so that it is not happenstance? "Yes" is the answer. It is built around the questions that so frequently swirl around us as leaders in the classic form of the *Who-What-Where-and-How* of learning. I leave out the *When* because in my experience, learning is a continuous process and not isolated to set periods. Learning must be a ubiquitous presence in our lives across all sets of knowledge – some with greater depth than others, of course – but all sets, regardless. We never know when those intuitive moments will flash across our minds and offer us insights that collate prior pieces of information into information and learning that move us and the organizations we lead toward additional knowledge.

So, the critical elements – aside from the *When* – are:

- *Who* needs to be involved in setting the stage for our learning?
- *What* is the best way for us to learn?
- *Where* are the best resources for supporting our learning needs and requirements?
- *How* can I sustain a culture of learning in my organization?
- *When* – if you must – should learning occur? *Think, all the time!*

The persistent leader is someone who continuously adjusts and adapts to the flow of their environment, from information and knowledge to the dynamics of their interactions with colleagues, as well as the response of markets and external constituents. Resistance to this continuous flow is not part and parcel of the persistent leader.[40] Rather, by setting aside the ego, the persistent leader allows the environment to share its knowledge and learnings. In sum, persistence is recognizing that the answers are not always within us, but most frequently out there in front of us.

Persistence takes time, energy, and an open attitude to maintain a focus on continuous learning. And, by continuous, I mean right up to the end. For example, I've discovered in recent years that, although I'm no longer serving as a leader of a large organization that presents new problems every day, I'm still learning. The "Aha" experience can come many years later if you are open and continuously scanning the environment for those little nuggets of insight. They're out there. Be persistent!

Creating a Culture of Learning – For the organization, creating a culture that fosters a tolerance for gathering knowledge from failures is essential. Leaders are the key to making that type of culture sustainable. Let's circle back to *Who* for a moment. You will note in the description of *Who* that the reference related to identifying those who must be involved are not "labeled" individuals (e.g., the boss, the director or manager, the CEO, etc.). Rather, the suggested approach is to foster an environment where it is acceptable for anyone to stand up to the powers that be and highlight a failure that may be on the horizon. The culture must absolutely create a psychologically safe environment for everyone in the organization, regardless of their role, position, or status.

So, how does one get that started in an organization? First, the persistent leader must insist that their organization develop a clear path for laying out *what* happened, not 'who did it,' when a failure has been identified. The lessons of Deming and all of his apostles on this topic are of paramount importance. Consistent reporting of failures – whether large or small – accompanied by a systematic analysis of the situation and forward-thinking solutions is essential. Such an approach will facilitate proactive problem-solving. The question then is: How does a leader instill such a culture in the organization? Here are the steps to consider:

1. ***Create an environment of openness through proactive team collaboration*** – As organizations move toward less hierarchical models, the use of teams is increasingly recognized as a responsible and reliable resource for rigorously reducing errors. Respect within the teams is a mandatory element.

2. ***Celebrate – Learn – Fix – Celebrate Again!*** – A continuous cycle that is bookended by celebrating is important. Failures must be uncovered first and put on the table. Learning from failures is the next priority, with the lessons openly shared within the team and then more broadly with the entire organization. Fixing the problem based on your team's recommendations, synthesizing the learnings, and

evaluating the solutions becomes the next priority and must be recognized as a part of everyone's job. Celebrating can follow as the solutions bring fruition to what <u>everyone</u> <u>has</u> <u>done</u> <u>together</u>.

3. ***Allow for experimentation*** – Not all problems will be resolved quickly, so creating an environment that promotes intelligent experiments for solving the problem is a prudent investment of time, energy, and resources.

4. ***Recognize that not all failures are blameless*** – Organizations need to define the expectations on where the boundaries or "rules of the road" are in terms of what is and is not acceptable. If these boundaries are clear and known to all, you will be amazed at the support you will receive for fostering a new culture.

5. ***Have the right people in the room*** – Too frequently, organizations assign the task of failure analysis to a subgroup who are tasked with defining *what* went wrong and *why*. While it can be very useful to have a defined group for organizing the analysis, it is crucial to have those who were part of the failure or have an understanding of the elements of the failure under review in the room as well when the analysis occurs. Otherwise, the analysis could result in an incomplete assessment, lead to finger-pointing, or misdirect the organization.

6. ***Recognize that there are different types of failure*** – Not all failures are alike. There are those of a "routine" nature. Some failures evolve as a result of the "complex" nature of a particular activity or initiative within the organization. And there are failures in the "frontier" where no person or organization has gone before (sort of like the Star Trek model). The individuals who must be involved, the types of information gathered to support the analysis, and how the analysis is disseminated within the organization may vary. But the process of detecting, analyzing, assessing, and defining remains the same for all three types.

Finding And Resolving Failure – Some failures are obvious. Consider these examples of obvious failures and the outcomes that were precipitated:

- Think about the large corporations or the rapidly evolving start-ups that suddenly announce a decision to move into Chapter 11 bankruptcy.

- Consider the person who is admitted to the hospital and has brain surgery because the wrong person was wheeled into the operating room where the neurosurgeon was ready to work (this actually happened).[41]

- How about the 2007 collapse of the Interstate bridge over the Mississippi River in Minneapolis, where the reasons related to the wear and tear on "gussets", the lack of appropriate inspection, and the temporary additional weight added to the bridge by construction equipment that had been parked on it.[42]

These are obvious examples of catastrophic failures, called forth into the public view, and easy to spot. In most cases, however, such failures could have been averted with earlier attention to underlying problems that, when they coalesced with other problems, turned into failure. While the preceding discussion on how to prevent failure is a critical formative function for any organization, the actual mitigation of future failures through detection and resolution is also a critical capability. Instituting a more formal approach is a highly effective strategy for creating a more reliable failure prevention program.

As I noted previously, identifying failure begins with culture – both organizational and personal. On the organizational side, a plethora of tools exists, many of which originated from the Total Quality Management initiatives that began in the 1960s and gained substantial momentum in the 1990s. Peter Drucker, Ph.D., [43] the famed management guru, was the inspiration for much of the movement. Through his efforts and those of his disciples, the corporate world began to embrace such interesting ideas as customer interviews to find out their perspective, implementing High-Reliability Organization (HRO) practices, event analysis, and a host of other efforts, which were all designed to identify the potential for failure much earlier. Countless examples are available if you're patient enough to search for the topic. The message for the Persistent Leader is to focus simultaneously on tools and culture. They are symbiotic. One without the other will not get you there. However, the lesson learned from these experiences is that even with the implementation of the right techniques, if the organization's culture does not embrace the information, change does not occur.

The DAAD Approach
A Formal Approach to Failure Identification
Detecting – Analyzing – Assessing – Defining

While a framework is useful for creating the proper culture for failure prevention, there is also a need for a more rigorous approach to *detection, analysis, assessment, and definition of failure* as a regular part of practice within the organization. The DAAD Approach offers such an approach. It is also very important to understand that *the DAAD Approach is not sequential but, instead, an integrated approach to failure identification and prevention.* Here are the key elements of the model.

Detection – How can you lead an effort to alter the culture of your organization to more easily detect failure in the future? The Society for Human Resources Management (SHRM) outlines in some detail the specific elements of effective approaches to failure identification and resolution.[44] The model outlined by SHRM contains ten areas for failure assessment and analysis. However, within the list, the DAAD Approach provides a good starting point for any leader working to develop a culture of failure awareness. To initiate the approach for shifting the culture, here are a few steps for getting started with detection:

- **Define and Declare Your Values** – Declaring your organization's or company's values is a critical first step. But it's not just identifying them. It's also posting the values, declaring them front and center on your website, regularly talking about them with your employees or members, and making the declared values a living part of the fabric of what people do each day at work or within your organization. Through such an approach, values will become evident. The next step to be clear in your value statement is to outline how "failure" is to be recognized, dealt with, and used as a force for "making things better".

- **Connect Culture, Strategy, and Workflow** – Too frequently, companies stop at the values stage and fail to move forward by not making failure detection an integral part of their strategy, goals, objectives, processes, and ongoing workflow. What does this mean? Integration starts not only with your outward declarations but also with how and who you hire, how and when you evaluate members of the workforce, how and for what you compensate your workers, and a host of other human resources-related issues. It is more than an HR function. It also includes the processes used in actually identifying, reviewing, and managing potential or real failure *opportunities* (NOTE: Failure should always be viewed from the lens of what Henry J. Kaiser, the ship-building titan, once said in describing problems or failures as "*...only opportunity in work clothes.*"

- **Celebrate Failure Identification** – Rather than hiding failure, the successful integration of failure detection requires bringing failure to the forefront of the organization so it can be discussed, reviewed, debated, dissected, and yes – even celebrated by you and the employees. A Persistent Leader will be at the head of the class in celebrating failure identification. There are numerous examples in both large and small companies where failure has become a celebratory event, driving improvements in development, operations, and deployment. Consider it.

Celebration, in itself, is probably one of the more challenging approaches for fostering a cultural shift that embraces failures. But it is also one of the most effective. In addition, it is an effort that extends across the organization from small groups involved in identifying failures to reports provided to management, to oversight by governance or the Board of Directors in such discussions. Furthermore, it is not just the what but the *how* of information sharing that is extended across the entire company.

- **Persistent Leaders Lead Through Failure** – There is nothing quite like having the CEO or one of the major leaders, or a *Persistent Leader* of a company, stand up in front of everyone and declare the value of failure detection. There's an old adage that is important to remember in this regard: *People watch what you do, not what you say*. While this is a truism, it is important to start with "say" and then follow through with the "do." It's a both/and situation! By stepping up, stepping in, and stepping out, the Persistent Leader helps make culture change real, relevant, and accountable to everyone in the organization. Go for it...

Analysis – Once the failure is identified and on the table, the next step is to conduct a root cause analysis. Root cause efforts – across all industries – are very disciplined and rigorous, with defined approaches that detail all the antecedent events preceding the actual failure, regardless of whether they seem important at the time. The right approach to analysis will lead to the right lessons (see the next chapter) and the right solutions to ensure that failure does not persist for that particular problem.

In the healthcare field, where I have worked as a senior physician executive, root cause analysis has become a requirement over time due to accreditation requirements. However, to date, within the healthcare community, while requirements may exist, the inculcation of true root cause analysis is often lacking, despite the complexity of the care delivery process. The same is almost assuredly true in other sectors as well. Why? It's often the result of what is described as a *fundamental attribution error (FAE)*, **correspondence bias**, or the **attribution effect**. These are "...the claim that in contrast to interpretations of their behavior, people place undue emphasis on internal characteristics of the agent (character or intention), rather than external factors, in explaining other people's behavior."[45] In essence, the effect is a tendency on the part of the participants conducting the failure analysis process to believe that what people _do_ reflects who they _are._ So, if the problem relates to a nursing problem, it is the nurses who are responsible. If it occurs during a surgical procedure, it's the doctor's. When, in fact, just the reverse could just as easily be true with further analysis. Similarly, if it relates to the acquisition of tools, it is the product acquisition team. If the problem is on the assembly line, it's the line workers. However, the reverse could also be true. The actual problem may lie elsewhere and should not be overlooked.

The important point in fostering appropriate failure analysis is to motivate the people in your organization. You must foster an approach that encourages everyone to get under the covers and go beyond first-order reasons (e.g., procedures weren't followed) to a more robust understanding of the second, third, and fourth-order reasons that contributed to the failure. How is this accomplished? _Teams!_ What kinds of teams is no doubt the next question? The obvious answer is to use interdisciplinary teams that hold a diverse set of skills, capabilities, and perspectives. And the obvious reason is to mitigate the potential for a fundamental attribution error. If you gather a group of engineers together, they will likely overlook the potential problems attributed to engineers. The same applies to product managers, doctors, and other professionals involved in delivering products for your company. A diverse set of overseers creates the opportunity for a diverse discussion that will ultimately result in a better debate and analysis of the situation.

Complex failures, in particular, require such an approach because the depth and breadth of these problems extend across the entire organization. They can also evolve from multiple events that occur in different departments or disciplines, or at different levels of the organization. Understanding what happened, how it happened, what can be done to prevent it from happening again, and the best approach for sharing the information system-wide requires a very detailed, interdisciplinary discussion and debate to reach a fruitful analysis.

The best example, which is often used in describing these types of problems, is the 2003 Columbia Shuttle disaster.[46] It is an event seared into the memory of many of us because the incident was streamed live on national television, but also because of who was on the shuttle and its purpose in the evolution of our space exploration. The analysis took a considerable amount of time on the part of a leading interdisciplinary team of astronauts, engineers, physicists, aviation experts, weather specialists, ground support personnel, and other involved disciplines, who spent months working full-time on the analysis to determine the cause of the Columbia disaster. The interdisciplinary team not only identified the first-order cause of the disaster (i.e., a piece of foam hitting the shuttle's leading wing edge during launch) but also the second-order causes.

Through the comprehensive approach applied by the team, it was determined that the *culture* at the National Aeronautics and Space Administration (NASA) was a leading second-order cause that, without the multi-disciplinary team, may never have been articulated. Specifically, the rigidly hierarchical, externally focused, schedule-oriented culture of NASA created a climate where engineers were silenced from speaking up about their solid concerns. So, it's clear that culture is intimately intertwined with failure analysis. Persistent leaders not only recognize the problem; they also deal with the problem! So, start with culture first.

Assessment – The generic definition of assessment is "...the evaluation or estimation of the nature, quality, or ability of someone or something." I offer a slight variation on a theme by adding "experimentation" to the definition so that assessment is broadly thought of as *evaluation, experimentation, and estimation* of... Why is that important?

The promotion of experimentation as part of the assessment process enables organizations to accelerate their efforts in defining a better product or providing a better service. The inclusion of experimentation is a critical component that the Persistent Leader needs to support and integrate into the ongoing strategy for improving the results of the organization. Why?

1. Because it requires resources.
2. It requires the acceptance of a high initial failure rate as the organization experiments with how/where/ to whom the product is delivered.
3. It requires piloting without perfect conditions to reflect the realities of the marketplace, and,
4. It can require cannibalization of existing approaches and/or products.

Definition – If the detection, analysis, and assessment are completed properly as outlined in the preceding pages, the ability of the Persistent Leader and their team to define the failure will be accomplished relatively easily. In essence, definition *per se* is a dependent variable that requires a foundation built on the other three components. It is, however, an essential step. Why?

By clearly defining the cause of failure and, equally importantly, sharing it openly and transparently throughout the company, change will occur. The underlying reasons that caused the failure in the first place are much more likely to be dealt with than if the above steps are not followed.

Finally, in adopting the DAAD model, the next step is to create an environment conducive to the Persistent Leader's *ability to deal* with failure, so that, ultimately, *success* is realized through acceptance. It all comes together with what John F. Kennedy, the 35th President of the United States, once said: *Learning and leadership are indispensable to one another.*

So, read on...

CHAPTER X

The Importance of Outreach Towards An Involvement Of Community

Coming together is a beginning.
Keeping together is progress.
Working together is success.

Henry Ford
... a thoughtful American entrepreneur
during the latter part of the Industrial Revolution
and a successful businessman and motivator

While the focus of persistence at this point has been on the six core elements that serve as the framework for effective, *sustainable* persistence, there is one more element that is critical as part of the underlying fabric of success on any persistent initiative. It involves the approach you take as a leader toward helping to weave the fabric of energy, commitment, and focus among the people who express interest in becoming part of your persistent mission, vision, and values. Furthermore, it involves the approach you will take toward engaging with those who are either skeptical, initially opposed, and frankly, obstreperous toward your persistent objective(s). Over the preceding pages, I've alluded to it but never laid it on the table. However, the approach you take as a leader with a persistent objective toward the community in creating the essential element or fabric of support is different for a community than for a team! I'm referring, of course, to the team you assembled as part of your persistent initiative. So, let's delve into the question of teams a bit deeper as an important area of understanding before applying the *Persistence Sextuplet*.

Harnessing the support, commitment, energy, and persistence of a team – in many respects, offers somewhat easier and quicker results toward accomplishing an initiative for several reasons. First, the team is recruited and organized around the particular persistent objective from their point of engagement to the initiative. They may view it as simply a paycheck at the beginning, but with work, support, and insight, team members become advocates for the persistent objective. Three core considerations differentiate team adherence to a persistent objective. First, projects and focused tasks or operations represent solo operations in the world of change and seldom give birth to sustainable persistence. Second, while building a successful team also requires the effective adoption of the six elements I've previously described, the implementation is different. And third, given the relatively smaller number of individuals involved, the diversity of perspectives on direction and approach toward implementation within a team is more frequently unified.

In contrast, developing and organizing a community in support of a persistent objective generally involves considerably more diversity. First, the sense of commonality of mission is often more diverse in the community than with a team. Why? Because the individuals coming to a particular initiative arrived from different vantage points, with different perspectives and often, different expectations. Integrating those variabilities requires a willingness to engage in more dialogue and debate to maintain a focus on mission or purpose. Second, at the tactical level, there is frequently a much higher number of perceived approaches where the energy must be captured and the approach modified for the overall benefit of the community.

When considering how to effectively utilize the core elements outlined in *The Persistence Factor*, a crucial question to address is the purpose or mission behind your persistent focus. While the concepts outlined can be applied to "teams," the greater use of these ideas is related to mobilizing, engaging, and energizing "communities" or "cohorts" of committed individuals who work together toward a particular objective with persistence.

Organizing a community focuses on empowering a group of often diverse individuals with varied perspectives to address shared issues, while recognizing that building collective power is a productive outcome in the pursuit of a persistent objective or goal. In essence, a diversity of overall goals, objectives, and approaches needs to be organized (See the table on "Differences in Approach to Persistence" on the following page), which provides an analysis of the differences between team and community approaches to persistence. Both require organization, but in different ways.

Collaboration Across the Board — As a philosophical first step in team development, team members must support one another, both professionally and personally. The reason is that the lines of demarcation between the personal and professional when pursuing a persistent objective are often de minimis. Besides, a more collaborative and supportive environment is also more resilient. Where does resilience come from? It is most often derived from the members of a group bonded by common objectives derived from living and learning from one another, sharing feedback, and motivating each other in both good and bad times.

DIFFERENCES IN APPROACH TO PERSISTENCE		
Task	**Community**	**Team**
Focus	Building a sense of collective identity, shared purpose, and capacity for action within a group of people who live in proximity or share a common interest.	Structuring a group of individuals to work collaboratively towards a specific project or organizational objective.
Goal	To empower community members to address issues, advocate for their needs, and create positive change within their community.	To achieve efficiency, productivity, and effectiveness in completing tasks and meeting goals.
Approach	Often involves grassroots organizing, building relationships, identifying local leaders, and developing strategies for collective action.	Often involves clear roles and responsibilities, effective communication, project management tools, and regular check-ins.
Key Elements	<ul><li>**Relationship Building:** Fostering connections and trust among community members.</li><li>**Leadership Development:** Identifying and empowering local leaders to take on organizing roles.</li><li>**Collective Action:** Encouraging residents to work together to achieve shared goals.</li><li>**Grassroots Participation:** Ensuring that all community members have a voice in decision-making.</li><li>**Long-Term Engagement:** Building sustainable community power and capacity for ongoing change.</li></ul>	<ul><li>**Clear Goals and Objectives:** Defining what the team needs to achieve.</li><li>**Defined Roles and Responsibilities:** Assigning tasks and responsibilities to team members.</li><li>**Effective Communication:** Ensuring that team members are informed and can communicate effectively.</li><li>**Project Management:** Using tools and techniques to manage projects effectively.</li><li>**Collaboration and Cooperation:** Fostering a positive and productive team environment.</li></ul>
Examples	Organizing a neighborhood association to address parking issues Forming a coalition to advocate for better public transportation Mobilizing residents to support a local school project.	Organizing a marketing team to launch a new product Forming a software development team to build a new application Creating a project team to implement a new system.

A recent PDF book, *More In Common*,[47] was released by an organization with a focused mission: "*...both short and longer-term initiatives to address the underlying drivers of fracturing and polarization, and build more united, resilient and inclusive societies.*" The opening lines on the organization's website are telling in terms of their focus by providing:

> "*Connection across lines of difference—or, simply put, connection between people who do not share the same backgrounds or beliefs—is at the heart of the challenge of overcoming social isolation, strengthening community life, and building an America where everyone can feel they belong.*"

The mission is laudable but increasingly difficult in a world where, despite our connectivity, we are frequently disconnected. Therefore, those who hold a persistent objective need to reach out to one another not only because of like-minded objectives and perspectives, but also for support and connectivity in the long game of persistence.

Capturing the Inherent Diversity of Skills and Perspectives in a Community – A team, whether developed de novo or inherited, brings together individuals with different backgrounds, skills, experiences, and capabilities, but who hold a common objective derived from background, experience, employment, or common perspective. This phenomenon is especially important when discussing the notion of teams in the setting of a persistent pursuit. Why? In large measure, it relates to how teams pursuing persistent objectives often arrive at that vantage point of working together for highly variable reasons but with a common objective. This diversity can often lead to more creative solutions, better problem-solving, and more innovative ideas compared to what a single leader might come up with on their own.

In contrast, a community often develops through common involvement in a cause or experience, which again brings together individuals with diverse backgrounds, skills, experiences, and capabilities, but who share a common objective derived primarily from an experience or a challenge to their long-held beliefs or perspectives. Their involvement is generally of a volunteer nature as well, which can interfere with consistent involvement in the overall persistent objective. While the individuals involved in a community may have differing objectives, they generally hold a common purpose that ties them together in their pursuit of the initiative with persistent energy. In such an environment, these important characteristics enhance adherence to the persistent objective:

- The casual observer will notice that the community members listen to one another.

- Some members of the community will actively engage with those who hold alternative perspectives, while others will not.

- Leaders – not leader – of the community must understand "why" people feel the way they do and what can be done to mitigate those feelings.

- Diverse thinking is allowed but can be challenged, thereby fostering more creativity among those involved in the persistent initiative, with the end result that potential solutions for reaching the persistent objective will often be more diverse.

> *The thing that lies at the foundation of positive change,*
> *the way I see it, is service to a fellow human being.*

Lech Walesa

Leader of the Solidarity Movement in Poland, widely
recognized for playing a central role in ending communist
rule and recipient of the Nobel Peace Prize

Acceptance of Shared Responsibility: When a community works together on a persistent objective, there is often discussion on areas where additional information is needed, resources are required, blockages to progress are experienced, and the like. Furthermore, leadership is often more diversified and diffuse. No single person will necessarily be in charge of the overall goal or objective; however, a smaller number of individuals may emerge as the lead spokesperson for the community. Through the use of shared information, decision-making, and leadership, the community involved in a persistent objective will be able to come to quicker, better, faster solutions. The approach of shared responsibility also prevents burnout by allowing the community to adapt or pivot more easily as new or unforeseen challenges arise. In essence, while each member of the community in a persistent initiative is allowed to contribute in their own way, through the use of their own experience and knowledge, and with their own perspective on the why of persistence, holding to the common objective is of key importance.

Furthermore, a community that accepts shared responsibility will very often offer up a more consensus-driven decision-making process because, as a "community," the participants are ready, willing, and able to challenge each other's ideas and consider a broad range of factors due to the inherent nature of collaboration. While decisions in a team with a designated leader may be quicker, they are not necessarily better. A decision by a community with a broad mandate for a particular direction is much more likely to maintain its focus and direction on behalf of the persistent objective.

Finally, an environment of shared responsibility also results in collective accountability. The members of the persistent community hold one another accountable in multiple ways, which more frequently prevents failures by individuals or small groups within the community, due to the broad consensus on objectives and the ultimate persistent goal.

These ideas provide a general framework for the difference between a team and a community with persistent objectives. In addition to these ideas, there are some common activity sets that generate support and involvement in both teams and communities. Those ideas include the following:

1. **Clear Vision & Goals** – A shared purpose is important for any persistent objective or goal. The individuals involved in the initiative should understand the community's overarching vision and goals. Clarity on this point ensures that those involved are also aligned and motivated toward achieving the same persistent objectives.

2. **Roles & Responsibilities** – Clearly defined roles help avoid confusion among the multitude of individuals aligned with the persistent objective. Over time, the development and implementation of a "coordinating team" will be needed to facilitate activity, engagement, resource management, and other common considerations associated with an evolving persistent objective.

3. **Effective Communication** – Regular communication through meetings, emails, and interaction sessions, including the use of collaborative tools, will assist in maintaining transparency and keep the committed members of the community informed. The leadership team must encourage "active listening" to ensure all voices are heard, all ideas can be shared freely without judgment, and openness to alternative approaches is actively considered.

4. **Trust & Respect** – Trust is the foundation of any high-performing group or community. When those involved in a persistent objective trust each other, they collaborate more effectively and feel comfortable taking risks and offering alternative approaches to reach the group's goals. Maintaining a community culture built on mutual respect for all perspectives ensures that the various values of individuals contributing to the initiative are respected and valued.

5. **Embracing Diverse Skills & Perspectives** – A community with diverse skills and perspectives will foster more innovative and better-equipped solutions to problems faced by the greater community in working on persistent objectives. While "diversity" has been disparaged in recent years, when encouraged, it will foster the involvement of more diverse thoughts and experiences from a variety of backgrounds that enrich the community and frequently lead to more creative solutions.

6. **Leadership:** Strong yet open leadership helps provide direction, solves problems, and keeps the community motivated toward reaching the ultimate, persistent objective. Leaders should not only be approachable

and supportive but also ready, willing, and able to accept diverse perspectives and advise on how to move forward toward a persistent objective. Think Nelson Mandela, Martin Luther King, and those who are capable of making tough decisions. That said, solo leadership is not the sole solution. Strong, diverse leadership, on the other hand, can drive vision, facilitate the acceptance of tough decisions, and help to maintain clarity on the ultimate, persistent objective. Finally, the leadership needs to offer the following three elements:

- **Flexibility and Adaptability**: Teams can more quickly adapt to changing circumstances, as they have a range of skills and expertise to draw upon. If one strategy isn't working, a team can quickly brainstorm alternative solutions, whereas a solo leader might not have the bandwidth or insight to switch approaches effectively.

- **Opportunity for Generating Ideas and Innovation**: A team offers more ideas and input during the decision-making process, which can lead to better outcomes. While a solo leader may rely on their judgment, a team can help fill knowledge gaps and bring fresh insights to the table.

- **Fostering Morale and Engagement**: People are often more motivated and engaged when they feel part of a community. It creates a sense of belonging and purpose. In contrast, remaining sequestered or insulated from societal issues or problems, despite holding a perspective on the need for change or modification in the approach being taken, can be isolating and lead to disengagement or dissatisfaction.

In sum, it's clear from the research on group connectivity and motivation that individuals holding a perspective for change also believe that connecting across differences through collaboration is the way forward for creating sustainable change. Maintaining a consistent perspective facilitates achieving the objective.

Furthermore, by providing an opportunity for interaction, discussion, and debate, those holding the persistence objective can facilitate those who "lack opportunity" for engagement to meet that need. Finally, developing, presenting, and fostering discussion around a persistent objective you may hold along with others is a task that may take time but will ultimately yield results.

CHAPTER XI

On Acceptance

*Acceptance of what has happened is an essential step
to overcoming the consequences of any misfortune.*

William James

An American philosopher and psychologist who was the
first educator to offer a psychology course in the United
States

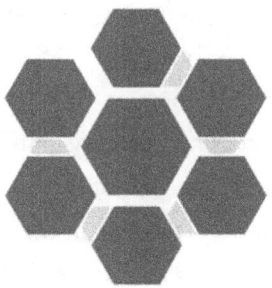

Sometimes learning comes quickly. Sometimes learning takes longer. And, sometimes, it seems to take forever. More often, learning is the accumulation of bits of information that, over time, become a clear message. The Persistent Leader ultimately hears these accumulated messages and moves to acceptance. So, in considering how to round out this section, I felt that the best way was to share a story – a very personal one – that exemplifies acceptance in ways that many detailed overviews and outlines cannot adequately convey.

The story begins in the fall of 1953, out on the western plains of Nebraska, when I was just a toddler. My family, like many German and Scandinavian (Swedes, Danes, and Norwegians) settlers in the western portion of the state, were farmers. They had moved to the area during a homestead land rush that spanned from approximately 1880 to 1910. Prior to that period, the overwhelming majority of immigrants to the United States made decisions to settle in the large urban centers that swelled in population throughout the 1800s following the Civil War. However, the German and Scandinavian immigrants differed in deciding to move to the rural areas of Wisconsin, Minnesota, the Dakotas, and Nebraska. Why? At the time, one immigrant begat another, as brothers reached back to brothers; uncles and aunts to nieces and nephews and the like, to encourage their relatives to move to America.[48] In addition, the environment and lifestyle they found in these areas were much more consistent with their homeland experiences. And...there was another reason – The Homestead Act!

Our family was like the classic description of homesteaders found in history books. My great-grandfather immigrated in 1888, eventually settling on a homestead near Gothenburg, Nebraska, in 1889. But it wasn't only him. It was his brother and several other relatives as well. Throughout the period, they flowed with the seasons, and eventually, my grandfather took over the farm. Like his father before him, he farmed wheat and corn without irrigation, which is a clear distinction from today's farming in the area.[49] In today's world, the farmers tap into the Ogallala Aquifer, a vast underground ocean extending from South Dakota into Oklahoma that provides the farmers with sufficient water resources (for the time being) to support irrigation, because that too is drying up with time. But, that's a different story! During the homesteading era, farmers were entirely dependent on the grace of good weather to quench the thirst of the parched land.

My father, like his father and grandfather, also became a farmer. However, by the time Dad came of age, the Homestead Act had expired, and the approach to owning a farm was to borrow money and repay it over time, which is what he did with the backing of my grandfather. Dad also learned the hows, whys, and ways of farming. He had grown up in the era when harvesting was done the "old" way using a sickle and a scythe. However, he was at the forefront of technology introduction into the farming enterprise with the introduction of tractors, combines, and a range of other tools used by farmers to make life easier in the pre-war era. And he adopted those new innovations on his farm. Rather than horses, he bought a tractor (actually, several) when they became more readily available following World War II. And, like his relatives before him, he practiced "diversified farming" by planting wheat and corn along with running some cattle, pigs, and chickens to stabilize the output of the farm. Our little farm seemed vast to me at the time. I remember as a small boy carrying lunch out to where the sound of the tractor was working in the field, as I discussed at the opening of this book. There are so many memories, but I digress...

In the fall of 1953, I had another type of "black" experience (not obesity 😊) that will become clear as you read on and which foreshadowed how I would manage the rest of my life. We started the season on a string of bad luck. First, we had locusts, which ate up everything in sight. I remember the locusts munching on the stalks of wheat as a little kid. As the locusts moved across the prairie, they literally cleared it of any grain. It was a devastating event before the era of pesticides. Nothing could be done. All was lost.

Then, in 1954, we had a drought.[50] It was overlaid by one of the worst, prolonged heat waves that the Midwestern community had experienced in decades. Again, like the locusts of the prior year, nothing could be done. All the crops were lost.

It was, therefore, with great anticipation that in 1955 we headed into yet another growing season. Everyone knew at the beginning of the year that it would be a make-or-break time for our farm, as it was in a precarious position with no crop results for the preceding two years. The series of events created a very tenuous financial situation for the farm, causing considerable anxiety. Long story short, the season went well. We came to the time of the wheat harvest in late August, and I remember the buzz of the family. We were all excited. The wheat was not only thriving, but its yield was also higher than normal.

Harvest started on one of those hot days in August when the neighbors gathered at our place to help, since "farming" was a community affair. The family gathered, neighbors joined, and friends were recruited to help with the harvest. Even a little boy of four had his place in the harvest event. My role was to stand in the seed hopper or the grain truck, which rolled alongside the combine, depending on what type of combine was in use at that particular time. As the grains of wheat were harvested and poured into the bin, my role was simply to stand there atop the grain and shovel the new granules of wheat into the corners of the bin. It was, in retrospect, a nominal but – shall I say – "important" role for educating me on the harvest process. Plus, I felt included as a member of the team. I did not substantially contribute much to the process, but the importance lay in teaching me to be a part of the family and serve as a member of the team as we worked together on the rather complex process of grain harvest. It was a crucial learning experience central to growing up on a farm.

I remember the day of our last family harvest because it was an inauspicious start to a very memorable day. It is imprinted on my mind despite the rust of nearly 70-plus years of aging. It was a very hot day late in the summer. Everyone was pitching in. Anyone who could assist with any part of the harvest effort was enlisted to participate.

I stood in the back of the harvester in the "seed hopper," and went to work. The sun was blazing. The day was hot, hot, hot! We were all sweating. And the sheer grit of our effort was clear from just looking at one another. My Dad was managing the back of the combine and supervising us boys in the harvester, and my Uncle was driving. There were others with assigned tasks as well, such as neighbors I didn't know, and my Granddad, whom I remember being there as well. I think he supervised, a role he managed quite well in his later years.

We were all working very hard, but what I remember next is a growing feeling of foreboding. We had been working in the field for an hour or two when, off on the horizon, we all noticed a very thin, dark, black line beginning to appear. It caught the attention of everyone. Still, we continued our work without interruption, with all of us occasionally looking up only to see it grow into an even larger swath across the entire sky. As we moved from one side of the field to the other, the black swath continued to grow until it began to cover the entire sky as a massive, black, thunderous cloud. Lightning emanated from the black cloud. It was an ominous sight, and soon became obvious to everyone that it was going to overtake us.

When the winds suddenly picked up, my Uncle and Dad conferred and announced that we were "...goin' in..." So, we left the combine in the field with the "seed hopper" full of grain, which we tried to cover with a tarp. We tied it down as best we could and then headed to the barn with the one load of grain we had harvested, parking it there. We then headed to the farmhouse, which was a short jaunt away.

It was at that point that I looked up. I remember seeing the large, black cloud as an angry, cacophonous storm. As we ran toward the porch, large pelts of rain dropped precipitously from the sky before turning into small pea-sized ice pellets. They then turned into marble-sized hailstones before becoming even larger, golf ball-sized hailstones. We stood on the open porch and watched. We watched in silence as the "amber waves of grain" in the field next to the farmstead were flattened to the ground, where just minutes before the wheat had been standing tall and ready for harvest. It was amazing! The storm did not seem to last more than a few minutes before it swiftly fled the scene, leaving a haphazard array of wheat stalks lying on the ground in a flattened mess. We all stood there in a posthumous stance, gazing out across the field in the quiet of the afternoon.

Throughout the entire period of the storm, I stood there holding my Dad's hand. I heard a soft shower of tears behind us somewhere. We stood there with our eyes transfixed on the horizon as the sun spread its warmth across the waste that lay before us. My Dad caressed my hand ever so softly as he stood there on the porch, a full 6'2" tall to my mere whatever.

It was at this point that I remember something that I will never forget. As I write this down, I get a bit emotional. I was just a small four-year-old kid wanting to grow up and be like Dad. He was holding my hand and, despite everything that was happening, he was gentle. The storm ended, and the winds ceased. The soft tears drew quiet, and a deathly silence overtook the porch. No one said a word. The silence seemed to go on forever, but was broken eventually by the following, which I will remember forever. There was a slight squeeze of my hand as my Dad, in his own quiet, earnest way, said,

"Well...

[followed by a short, several-second pause]

...I guess we should get on with the rest of our life."

In the end, we lost the farm. It was a change that had repercussions not only for Dad but for everyone in our family and the extended family. Those words have echoed at the core of my being for many, many years. He recognized the implications. It was not a picture of neglect. It wasn't necessarily a failure either. And for sure, it wasn't for lack of trying. It was simply circumstances. In my mind – as I look back – it was the penultimate statement of acceptance. And, with that one little comment, we got on with the rest of our lives... It has been a recurring theme in my life that when a failure occurred, over which I had little or no control, I would say to myself: "Well, I guess I should get on with the rest of my life."

But there's a second part of the lesson that is also very important. He persisted! That singular experience has resonated with me over the decades and become a bellwether reminder that continues to ring periodically in my life experiences. So, it is with persistence. It comes back around periodically. Disappointments, disillusionment, frustrations, lack of success, defeats, and even outright failures are a part of life. So, the singular lesson is that we must learn to adapt to life's experiences with a circle of persistence that embraces learning and acceptance. That's the reason I have dubbed this book *The Persistence Factor*. Because "persistence" is a key "factor" in our survival in life and the experiences we entail.

So, what are the acceptance lessons learned from this story? It seems to me that there are a couple of notable thoughts that percolate to mind, including:

1. **Acceptance of failure – when fully embraced – recognizes the reality of the situation.** When we can change something – we should do it. When we can't, we should accept it but learn from it as an important next step.

2. **Acceptance means understanding the results.** At some point, the Persistent Leader must accept the declared results of the failure. Not all problems can be rectified immediately. In some cases, the better option is not to "go at it again" or even to attempt to modify your approach while continuing down the same course. In some cases, accepting the reality of failure is as important as understanding it.

3. **Acceptance in one era does not mean acceptance in all eras.** Timing can be everything. The first smartphone was introduced in 1992 by IBM as the "Simon Personal Communicator" and was followed in 2000 by an Ericsson touchscreen device, the R380 Smartphone. It combined Personal Digital Assistant ("PDA") functionality with mobile phone capability. How many people bought one of these devices? Nada, said I, the nerdy guy who wrote this book... But, somewhere in a lab far, far away, a researcher did not walk away nor languish. They continued their work and eventually developed the platform for introducing the Apple iPhone – a device that has altered the course of communication history worldwide. Need I say more? Timing can be everything!

4. **Remember, this is your journey!** One element of the Persistence Journey that has become increasingly clear to me as I've grown older is that life is our journey. Persistence in one part of life may be folly in another. Think about the physical elements for a moment. The physical capabilities of a 30-year-old are quite different than those of a 70-year-old. Therefore, preparation for a marathon or even leading a corporation for the Persistent Leader requires an entirely different set of resources at different eras of one's life. The same applies not only to the physical but also to the emotional side of life. As a Persistent

Leader, do I want to "change the world," or, would I rather turn my attention to "enjoy the world"? The set of requirements and resources needed for accomplishing one's objectives in each situation is vastly different.

5. **Define your persistence in the present context.** Finally, acceptance requires the Persistent Leader to understand and fully embrace their context. This is perhaps the most difficult element of successful persistence. Too often, leaders persist when, in fact, true acceptance would encourage them to accept failure and move forward. This is difficult. This can be troubling. This is reality. When to call the question requires integrating all the lessons that the Persistent Leader has embraced over their lifetime of experiences.

Which brings us to *understanding...*

CHAPTER XII

Then Comes Understanding...

It's not that I'm so smart.
It's just that I stay with problems longer.

Albert Einstein

Understanding is built on a triad of learning, forgiveness, and patience. To begin the journey of true understanding, you must first recognize that you failed. Are you willing to step forward with that admission? Learning from failure is the second step. But the most important step of all is to develop an understanding of why you failed so that you can move forward. Early in his career, James Burke developed an attitude of "learning" followed by "understanding" that stood the test of time for him and the company that he led – Johnson & Johnson.

FORTUNE Magazine[51] did a profile of Burke back in 1988, in which they described an incident that set the course for his contributions to the company for decades. Burke had two different service points with the company. His first stay with Johnson & Johnson (J&J) didn't last very long after his initial arrival in 1953. He left after only one year because, as he described it: "The company was centralized and stifling and I was bored." He was in many respects an entrepreneur trapped inside a bureaucratic organization – an experience that many of us can relate to from our personal histories. Burke recalls that J&J "...did not have a new-products division, and when I left, I suggested we should have one."

His departure didn't last that long. It was only a short three weeks later that Burke was back at J&J because the organization had listened to his criticism and created a new products division. He was then asked to lead it. So, in the entrepreneurial style he enjoyed, Burke went about the journey of developing new ideas and products. One of his innovative products was a chest rub for children that was an abysmal failure. When he was summoned to the Chairman's office, he walked in fully anticipating that he would be let go again. However, General Robert Wood Johnson started the meeting by asking, "Are you the one who just cost us all that money?" Burke affirmed that he was the culprit with a nod of the head. The General then replied, "Well, I just want to congratulate you. If you are making mistakes, that means you are making decisions and taking risks. And we won't grow unless you take risks." It was a lesson that stood with Burke throughout the remainder of his tenure at J&J.

In November 1976, Burke received the ultimate J&J accolade when it was announced he would become the new CEO. A short time after that point in 1982, the integrity of the company was challenged by the Tylenol capsule poisoning with cyanide. His response came directly from the company's credo, which hung on the walls of the corporate offices, declaring that the "first responsibility" of the company was to its customers, then to its employees, management, communities, and stockholders – in that order. He held the credo and recalled Tylenol products by pulling all the capsules and tablets from the shelves of all stores and having them destroyed.

Through his understanding of what the J&J credo meant, he was able to lead the company through the crisis and on to recovery. Within one year, Tylenol regained 85% of its market share, and by the mid-1980s, it had made a complete recovery.

Failure is only bad if we do not understand it or learn from it. Failure can be a good thing. Alas, the mantra among many venture capital firms that fund early-stage start-ups is "fail early." With appropriate review, failure can mitigate further investments in initiatives, activities, or strategies that are moving in the wrong direction. Furthermore, failure in an early context can help identify where changes made early on can prevent needless waste down the road. Either way, value is created. The lessons learned from these trials by fire are that failure can sometimes be bad, but it can often be inevitable, at least to some degree, and that failure can even be a good thing.

The difficulty in learning from failure is that it is not like opening a book and simply reading the results. To be effective at "learning" from failure, your organization needs to possess the right *culture*, embrace the right *attitude*, and pursue the right *activities,* which represent the trifecta of effective learning from failure. It also means that your organization needs to move beyond not meeting the established protocols or guidelines as the reason for failure. Without this type of focus, learning can devolve into simply engaging in a blame game of *who did what wrong when*. Learning in such an environment does not occur primarily because it creates a culture where hiding the results is the name of the game. If you are hiding the results, little learning will occur.

Ultimately, it is essential to recognize that not all failures are equal. There are some failures that we can prevent. Some are process-related. And there are others that Sim Sitkin, Ph.D., of Duke University Fuqua School of Management, describes as "intelligent" failures.[52] What do I mean by each of these three types of failures?

- **Preventable Failures** – These are failures that occur when an organization has put together carefully crafted processes for routine operations that need to be followed to support a sustainable outcome or result. Much has been written about these types of failures. In particular, for the healthcare field, Atul Gawande's book, *The Checklist Manifesto,* provides a comprehensive overview of the value of monitoring for preventable failures. Another equally valuable approach is the much-vaunted *Toyota Lean Six Sigma* model, which has been adopted by a diverse array of industries where continuous learning is the mantra – even from very small discrepancies in defined processes.

- **Progression Failures** – I use the term "progression" because these types of failures often emanate from defined processes, but then at some point, the work or questions move into areas where there is uncertainty or a lack of definition. The preventable failures become progressive failures. There are numerous examples of situations where the protocol or algorithm ends, but the problem persists due to unforeseen issues that arise in the moment. The importance of these types of failures is that they provide your organization with new information on how to build a better process. Therefore, capturing these bits of failure is a very important step toward fostering improvement, achieving efficiency, and improving quality.

- **Intelligent Failures** – These are the types of failures that occur when an organization intentionally tries something new or experiments with its approach to solving a problem. It could involve building an entirely new approach to business from the outside in, where the old model of business is discarded in favor of new approaches. Did Uber make mistakes in the beginning? You bet! How about the drug companies as they pursue the development of new drugs and compounds that have never been used before in treatment programs? Again, much of the time. These are all "intelligent" failures. While the project or activity may not succeed, the company gains knowledge and experience in solving problems. Organizations that are effective at "intelligent" failures use the additive effect of all the failures to create solutions that would never have been realized without the intentionality of failing.

The result of the failure message is that while we can fail on the outside, if we learn from our persistence on the inside, we will succeed. It's a difficult lesson. Society often does not accept it. But we need to hold it as a gift to *fail forward*.

The second element of understanding that is often forgotten in discussions about persistence is the act of forgiveness. Forgiveness is the deliberate decision to put aside your *feelings,* regardless of whether it is deserved or not. It is not condoning or excusing errors or offenses, but is recognizing that to fully understand, we need to let go. If we hold the door closed too tightly, if we fail to hear the information that others want to share with us, if we will not allow the reasons and rationale of an argument to see the light of day, the blocks we create will prevent a true understanding of the situation. By forgiving, we can release the corrosive anger and distilled hostility we hold inside, which prevents us from gaining a true understanding of a situation, a person, or an event.

Forgiveness circles back to those who fail in so many different ways. The purpose is not to justify the mistakes but to understand them. By understanding them, we create an environment that fosters a celebration of understanding, which can be deeply embedded in the corporate culture. The result of learning with a healthy dose of forgiveness is to foster a far deeper understanding of any situation than pure analysis might offer. It's the yin and yang of understanding – data and feeling. The combination is very powerful.

Finally, the third element of the triad, which provides the foundation for understanding, is patience. The best way I can think of to introduce this most important element for fostering understanding is to share...*The Story of the Butterfly*.

The Story of the Butterfly

A man found a cocoon of a butterfly.
One day a small opening appeared.
He sat and watched the butterfly for several hours
as it struggled to squeeze its body through the tiny hole.
Then it stopped, as if it couldn't go further.

So the man decided to help the butterfly.
He took a pair of scissors and
snipped off the remaining bits of cocoon.
The butterfly emerged easily but
it had a swollen body and shriveled wings.

The man continued to watch it,
expecting that any minute the wings would enlarge
and expand enough to support the body,
Neither happened!

In fact, the butterfly spent the rest of its life
crawling around.
It was never able to fly.

What the man in his kindness
and haste did not understand:
The restricting cocoon and the struggle
required by the butterfly to get through the opening
was a way of forcing the fluid from the body
into the wings so that it would be ready
for flight once that was achieved.

Sometimes struggles are exactly
what we need in our lives.
Going through life with no obstacles would cripple us.

We will not be as strong as we could have been
and we would never fly.

What Persistent Leaders learn is that the answers to failure are not always fully evident. The data may not always be sufficient or clear enough to fully define the situation. The interpretations, even with the use of a multidisciplinary team, may not always be correct or may languish in unresolved conclusions because the selected team never really functioned as a cohesive unit, but rather simply as a collection of experts. The result is that to make sense of failure, we need to hold the tension of the inconsistencies together in our minds.

There is often a paradox in the learning process. I frequently hear from colleagues and individuals who aspire to be leaders that the lessons learned are like "scars on their backs." The implication is that they failed for one reason or another but learned from the experience. To become an excellent learner often requires you to be excellent at failing, not just once but many times. If there is one consistency about my career that I am willing to share later in my life, where I was previously more reticent, it relates to the failures that were often better teachers than the successes. The obvious tension of holding, considering, and adapting to the inconsistency and contrary nature of learning and failing in the same experience is a paradox. But it is a paradox worthy of embracing. It is through holding the continuous tension between learning and failure that understanding evolves.

I realize that this may sound Zen-like. The wisdom of the religions is an element that Persistent Leaders need to consider bringing to the forefront for facilitating understanding. The stories and aphorisms of all the great religions are worthy of consideration in this context, whether they are Hinduism, Confucianism, Taoism, Sufism, Zen, Buddhism, the Jewish prophets, Jesus, and the Desert Fathers and Mothers, or any others that have called you over time. The parables and lessons from these points of view can offer mortar for holding our experiences together in a reasonable facsimile for considering our experiences and drawing upon them to foster and support true understanding.

Now that I've gotten philosophical, let's explore the next important consideration...

CHAPTER XIII

The Pursuit of Mindfulness

Mindfulness is not about getting rid of distractions or judging
them, but about being present for whatever is here,
whether we like it or not,
whether we planned it or not.

Sean Fargo

a mindfulness teacher and the founder of Mindfulness
Exercises, dedicated to making mindfulness accessible to
everyone via the web.

An important element in helping the Persistent Leader manifest their dreams
is maintaining a mindful presence. For the hard-charging, focused, resolute
person, this can be a very difficult – if not often neglected – part of the
armamentarium for the _**effective**_ (i.e., double underlined, italics, bolded,
please pay attention) Persistent Leader. There are numerous books and other
resources available on mindfulness, so I won't attempt to make this chapter a
comprehensive compendium on the topic. Rather, the intent is how, as
Persistent Leaders, we can take an approach toward mindfulness as a resource

for bringing work and life together in harmony with our approach toward persistence.

Where does this begin? It seems to me that it all starts with the simple things in life. Zen master Thich Nhat Hanh teaches us that there is wisdom derived from the ceremony and meditation of tea. In many respects, it is the Buddhist parallel to the Christian Eucharist or the Jewish Passover.

But let's not get lost in the religious metaphors. Rather, the importance is what he offers as an introduction to the Tea Ceremony.

Consider the following:

You must be completely awake in the present to enjoy the tea.

Only in the awareness of the present can your hands feel the pleasant warmth of the cup.

Only in the present can you savor the aroma, taste the sweetness, and appreciate the delicacy.

If you are ruminating about the past or worrying about the future, you will completely miss the experience of enjoying the cup of tea.
You will look down at the cup, and the tea will be gone.

Life is like that.

If you are not fully present, you will look around, and it will be gone.
You will have missed the feel, the aroma, the delicacy, and beauty of life.
It will seem to be speeding past you. The past is finished.

Learn from it and let it go.
The future is not even here yet. Plan for it, but do not waste your time worrying about it.
Worrying is worthless

When you stop ruminating about what has already happened, when you stop worrying about what might never happen, then you will be in the present moment.

Then you will begin to experience joy in life.[53]

The Tea Ceremony is but one technique for helping the Persistent Leader to broach the broader field of mindfulness. In many different settings, mindfulness has proven to be an effective approach for reducing stress, enhancing attention, retaining focus, and improving retention. There is considerable accumulating research that suggests that engagement in regular mindfulness exercise can alter the biochemical and physiological responses of our body and brain. Studies have shown, for example, that mindfulness practices can strengthen the connections between the prefrontal cortex (i.e., the thinking brain) and the limbic system (i.e., the reactive brain), supporting increased self-reflection and self-regulation in response to stress. Such connectivity can play a critical role in learning, memory, and retention. You can even do a small experiment in the confines of your home.

Try this test and see what kind of results you get:

- First, take your pulse.
- Then, turn on some calming music with the lights turned down low.
- Assume a comfortable, neutral sitting position.
- Place the back of your hands on your knees in an open position.
- Close your eyes.
- Breathe in and out slowly while maintaining your focus on your breath as it flows over, across, and through your nostrils.
- Let your mind drift. Let your mind take you to a quiet place. I often travel to a virtual glen surrounded by trees. Sit there and absorb the present.
- Do this for 5 minutes, although 10 minutes is even better.
- Take your pulse again. It will most likely be slower.
- See the connection between your physical self and your mental self?

Several techniques are available to support your efforts in engaging in mindfulness. Here are just a few suggestions to get you down the path of more comprehensive solutions and approaches available in the mindfulness literature:

1. **Contemplation** – As I was working on this chapter, I took a short break from writing to look out the window. I live on a bay off the Eastern seaboard on the coast of Maine. It's quite beautiful here. In fact, as a North Dakotan, I can tell you that it is outrageously beautiful (but so is North Dakota in a different way). I frequently tell people that Maine and the people who live here are just like North Dakota – except they have mountains, the ocean, and trees. But...again, I digress. Back to looking out the window. At a point where I had become stuck on what to say about "mindfulness," I looked out the window rather spontaneously and stared at the tide, which was beginning to come in. After about 10 minutes, I realized that I was still standing there, but the clarity of what I wanted to say was top of mind. So, I sat down and spontaneously wrote this chapter. Such is the value of contemplation – about what does not matter. Contemplation is often enough to create clarity of thought.

2. **Conduct a Kamau Bell Exercise** – Kamau Bell is the host of CNN's Emmy Award-winning television show, *United Shades of America*. He engages in difficult conversations with groups of people with whom he might not normally engage. For example, as a black comedian, he has talked with members of the Ku Klux Klan and even attended one of their rallies. These are the types of conversations that we frequently try to actively ignore or push aside. However, there is tremendous learning that can occur through engaging in such discussions. By opening ourselves up to alternative viewpoints, perspectives, and vantage points, we can look at the world around us in new and different ways. Often, alternatives to our held viewpoints can evolve from such encounters. Consider it...

3. **The Guided Raisin Exercise** – A common mindfulness exercise involves guiding a group through a focused contemplation of a raisin. Participants are instructed to observe it closely by looking at it, touching it, smelling it (both directly and by cupping it in their hands), and feeling it with different parts of the body, not just their fingers. They then taste, chew slowly, and finally swallow it, either in pieces or whole. The goal is to fully engage with the raisin, using all the senses, and foster heightened focus, awareness, and presence throughout the experience.

4. **Journaling for Me, Myself, and I** – Although I did not originally know it was related to mindfulness, I've been engaging in this approach episodically since I was in medical school. When I look back on the writings from earlier eras, I'm always amazed at how the reality of what I was feeling comes to the forefront as a memory for me. Those periods when I wrote – sometimes in the middle of class and often late at night – represented times when I turned inward to a state of silence and contemplative self-listening, which lasted from a few minutes to an hour or more as I wrote what was on my mind. The part I added in my latter years was to pause and ask myself periodically, "What am I trying to say here?" The question allowed me to step back from the moment and the intensity of the writing experience, enabling me to define more clearly what I was thinking and what lay behind the words being scripted on the page. Such an approach helps one define the issue more clearly behind the obvious words.

5. **Simply Reading** – One of the major problems I have in life is what some might call a case of severe book acquisition syndrome, or hoarding. But, from my perspective, it's not so much hoarding as it is the emphasis on acquiring. I easily share. That's because I have so much to share 😊. As I write this paragraph, I have 59 unread books on the table behind me, another 5 books on the floor next to me, and countless numbers of magazines and journals spread across the floor

– all awaiting my attention. And, this does not include the two large books I am presently carrying around in my briefcase for quick reads on planes or in times of waiting. In large measure, I blame the ease of acquisition on Amazon.com and how it has become my "go-to" source for the latest ideas, materials, books, and such to quench my thirst for information and knowledge. The important part, however, is that I will eventually get to all those books. I've been in a similar situation before, but I managed to get through the accumulation. Reading for me is not simply a process of acquiring information. Rather, it is an approach toward gaining a better understanding of the world around me. The diversity of opinion I can distill as a result of reading very diverse opinions and perspectives has allowed me, over the years, to take a more measured approach toward "understanding".

6. **Staying Silent** – This is a great exercise. Again, I use the inward and outward-bound tide as my approach, either at dawn or dusk. I use those times (mostly dusk 😊) because they are generally periods of overall silence in the great outdoors where I live. I sit, looking at the bay, and remain silent for a set – often lengthy – period, allowing my mind to drift and thoughts to dissipate. When the darkness surrounds me, I continue to sit. It's a great way to cleanse the mind. It is very similar to contemplation as described above, but with less intent, less focus, and a penultimate emptiness of thoughts.

These are just a few techniques I have found helpful to begin the process of mindfulness in my life. Like any exercise, it simply takes effort to get started. It takes a commitment to continue.

Enjoy the journey...

CHAPTER XIV

On Reflection and Release

The real man smiles in trouble, gathers strength in distress,
and grows brave by reflection.

Thomas Paine

Let's start with the question: What is reflection? One interpretation is simply that a body or surface of light, heat, or sound is thrown back toward the source without absorption, such as the reflection of "light" from a mirror, or "heat" from an oven. A second use of the word reflection is that it represents serious thought or consideration, as in, "She needs time for reflection." Both are apropos in many respects to the question of how this relates to the concept of the Persistent Leader. We often need the first type of reflection to get our attention. The second type of reflection causes us to stop, absorb, and consider what is before us. Both types of reflections – it seems to me – are two sides of the same coin, to adopt an overused metaphor.

Upon considering how best to describe "reflection and release", I decided to share a story to set the stage. This is based on a true story I alluded to in Chapter VIII. It reflects upon me in ways that are not necessarily the ones I would normally share. However, the story provides a compelling backdrop for the ideas I'm trying to convey.

Once upon a time, there was a young man who had some notable success early in his career. Let me be honest. The story is about me! I was accepted into the residency of my choice at a major eastern program, which rescued me from the confines of my Midwestern roots. While it was a great experience, I quickly realized that the Midwest was a wonderful place, and when my former Dean called me up to recruit me to "come back home", I jumped at the opportunity. It was an opportunity to make a difference. You see, "making a difference" had become the hallmark of my intentionality related to work and home life.

Throughout these early years, I served in several local, statewide, and national roles, which continued to advance my career but often left me alone, on the road, and away from my family in places both far and near. Such was the life of a vagabond executive who was slowly making a name for myself not only here but abroad as well. I accumulated all sorts of recognition as a "future leader to watch," someone whose opinion was necessarily sought on areas of my expertise and who was likely to make a difference in health care.

As the years passed, I continued to advance up the corporate ladder. I was increasingly called upon to participate in a variety of gatherings – both professional and social – to offer thoughts, perspectives, ideas, and solutions for addressing problems. And yet, throughout this entire period, there was a sense of emptiness that filled my spirit. But I most frequently ignored the callings of emptiness by filling it with food and drink. It was a good way to cover the problem. It was so good that over time, I accumulated enough weight to tip the scales at 398 lbs. When asked about my size, I frequently commented that I had "...become a big boy." Or, I would jokingly note that I was "no longer a linebacker for the Green Bay Packers, no one got in my way." I would then smile and pat my tummy.

To hide the transgression of consuming too much food, I started wearing black. Besides, I found that it was a great color – or, lack thereof – for covering up weight gain. As I progressed through the eras, I adopted a "slightly larger Steve Jobs look," characterized by a black, collarless sweater, paired with a black suit and black shoes, and no tie. My dress was all black, and I felt that I could go anywhere from community picnics to The White House and everything in between, from meeting community folks to the Presidents of nations far and wide. I adopted the moniker of serving my community as the "Johnny Cash of Health Care." I competed with another colleague (who shall remain nameless, except to the healthcare community) who wore all black, except that he was slender and wore an open-collar shirt. Regardless, the style took hold, and many people never saw me in anything but all black, except for the small whisk that adorned the lapel on my suit with a story describing "why" that you've read earlier in Chapter VIII. I stirred things up! Now, hopefully, the story is not getting too long. One day, I was at a meeting that I had helped to organize, where I had invited a sitting U.S. Senator with whom I'd done a lot of work – to join the group and offer his opinion on the future of health care. The group gathered, and I introduced the Senator, who took the podium, where he recognized the many people he knew in the meeting, went around the room, and noted their presence. After five or six such "hellos" and "good to see ya's," he got to me and said, "It's so good to see you, Kevin. It's been a while. Why...you are twice the man you used to be." (drum roll, cymbal crash). It was a bit of a deflating experience.

Later that evening, the Senator, one of our mutual friends, and a colleague who was a nutrition expert, sat together at dinner. The casual conversation slowly drifted back to the afternoon and somehow shifted to our friend as the nutrition expert began discussing his new book on dietary control. In a rather abrupt way, the Senator looked at the nutrition expert and then turned to me, saying in a friendly, direct way, "You know – you've become fat!" "Fat! Really?" I replied. "Yeah, fat!" he responded without much thought. So, I turned to the nutrition expert and asked,

"What should I do? I've tried every diet known to man without any success."

After some discussion, it became apparent that the nutrition expert was willing to help me by offering the opportunity for me to call his cell phone after taking a walk every day. At the time, I lived in the hills just north of San Francisco, which provided an excellent venue for walking, and the weather was always perfect (except in summer, of course). So, I started walking, and within a couple of weeks, I had to stop. Why? Because I developed bilateral stress fractures from walking and being overweight, markedly overweight, I might add.

The essence of the story is that for the first time, I realized I was truly "fat" and I wanted to do something about it. It was my "Aha!" moment, where it had become obvious not only to others but also to me as well.

I then underwent an intensive period of reflection, during which I considered the options. I searched the literature, talked with several colleagues and experts in the field of obesity, and truly pondered my predicament for the first time. After some soul searching, I landed upon the more radical approach of a new type of bariatric surgery, where, due to the surgery, the individual could neither consume nor absorb too many calories. It was a procedure that offered promising – and, more importantly, permanent results. So, I proceeded.

The result was that after about 18 months following the procedure, I had dropped from my zenith of 398 lbs. down to a mere 175 lbs., which at a height of 6'2" meant I was quite slim. With a whole new set of black clothes (☺), I became a rejuvenated person. The energy that I had assumed was gone forever returned. No longer did people cross their fingers as I walked down the aisle on an airplane, hoping that I would not sit near them. I found that people interacted and engaged with me in entirely different ways than they had previously when I was "a big boy". The askance looks were also gone. I had a new life and embraced it fully. With added energy, I renewed my efforts to "make health care better."

The experience is true and resulted from considerable reflection on my part on how I was leading my life. I share the story not only because it is true but also because it represents the "Reflect and Release" approach I wanted to convey as an especially critical element of the persistence continuum that is too often missing. As Thomas Paine suggested, I smiled at the trouble I was in and gained strength by looking at the distress directly and unashamedly. I then exhibited sufficient bravery to turn my body over to a surgeon conducting a new type of procedure with the anticipated hope of finally dealing with the obesity problem. Yes, I even started using the word "obesity" to describe the problem to others outside of my close circle of friends.

In essence, by releasing my control over my situation, I allowed others to help me, and ultimately, made a huge difference in my life by not only extending it but also making it better day by day. "Making it better."...Why? Because I had developed hypertension, diabetes, and untold other problems as well, which accompanied my obesity. It was through reflection and release that I moved in a _new_ direction, coming to a _new_ understanding that ultimately allowed me to resolve a problem in my life. Such is the value of reflection and release.

Finally, the importance of learning when to "release" should not be lost on the reader. Serving as a Persistent Leader – emphasis on the "persistence" part – is often one of the impediments to recognizing when you have hit the wall, so to speak. It is the point where continuing down the same course, using the tools you've accumulated through experience, adopting and integrating all of the processes described in the previous chapters, and using the knowledge you've gained are recognized as insufficient variables in helping you to solve the problem. It is at that point where we – as Persistent Leaders – all need to _release_. We need to let go. For the Persistent Leader, this is one of the most difficult tasks. It is so difficult that far too many Persistent Leaders fail to accept it, only to fail yet again. Letting go can be very powerful. Scary but powerful. And, it can help you set a modified direction through reflection and release!

Good luck...

Then, The Need To

Repeat

The Cycle Again...and Again...and...

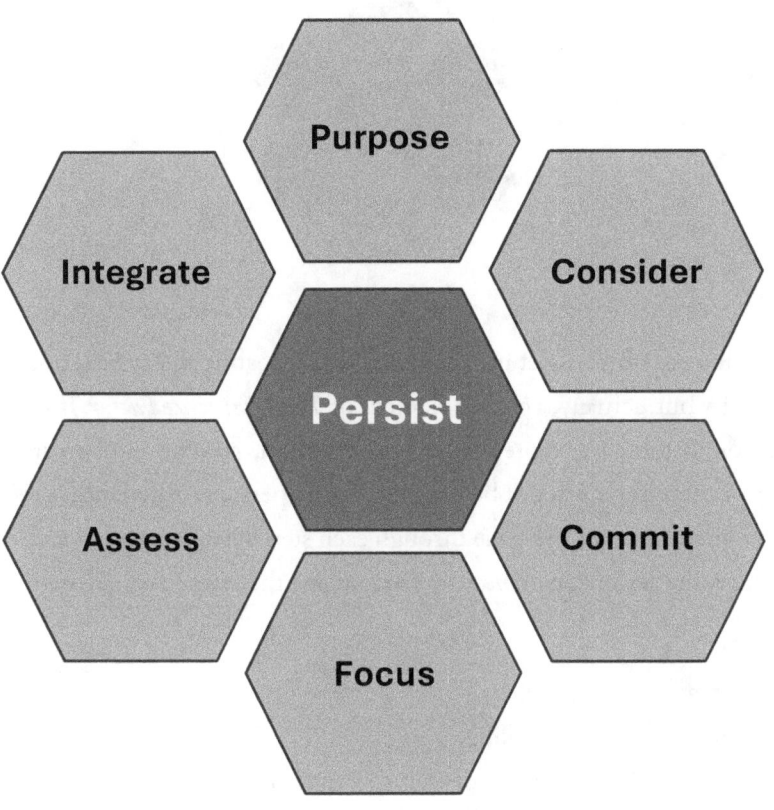

CHAPTER XV

Integration By Repeating The Cycle With Forgiveness

The weak can never forgive.
Forgiveness is the attribute of the strong.

Mahatma Gandhi

In case it's not obvious, let me point out that repeating the cycle is not only a possibility but, actually, a central element of *The Persistence Factor*. If we don't go through the cycle of review, reconsideration, revision, and redirection, many of our efforts will not be possible. In my personal experience, a regular, ongoing repetition of the cycle through each step is a mandatory exercise that facilitates the act of *persistence*! By engaging in the review, we are better able to...

Contemplate our purpose,

Consider a shift in our thinking,

Recommit to our conclusions or shift to alternatives,

Re-focus our time and energy on the persistence objective,

Addressing our vulnerabilities and/or successes; and,

Integrating what we've learned and

And, repeat the cycle again, if necessary...

Furthermore, it's also important to adopt an approach of self-forgiveness. When our objective of persistence becomes embedded, the process of shifting our focus and energy can often be difficult. And the difficulty stems from our unwillingness to admit errors in our thinking or our misaligned understanding of the problem or situation, which represents the focus of our persistent energy.

But, before we go much further, it's important to start our examination of persistence reconsideration with a definition of forgiveness. The Wikipedia definition is as follows:

> **Forgiveness** is the intentional and voluntary process by which a victim undergoes a change in feelings and attitude regarding an offense and lets go of negative emotions such as vengefulness with an increased ability to wish the offender well[54].

Forgiveness is not simply disallowing that an action was not wrong and, therefore, does not need forgiveness. It's not excusing, forgetting, pardoning, or reconciling. Rather, it is the active step away from those feelings that can cloud our perspective on a situation or a person, as well as the thoughts we hold about them or the situation.

So, why a discussion on forgiveness?

My intention in concluding The Persistence Factor is to focus on forgiveness, particularly self-forgiveness. The process is based on my experience, whereby the lack of forgiveness of others as well as ourselves diminishes our ability to persist! It drags us down. The lack of forgiveness keeps us focused on the wrong issues. It does not allow for change to occur, and change is a constant in today's world. If we do not forgive, we hold a situation or perspective constant, which prevents growth and development. Persistence is all about growth and development – both of ourselves and those around us.

There are many, many stories of forgiveness. The vast majority seem to focus on forgiving individuals who have wronged other individuals. And, while these stories are compelling, they don't quite capture the essence of what is the important element for leaders who are engaged in a persistent objective and reach the point where they need to embrace self-forgiveness. Rather, the important requirement for the persistent leader is to offer a humble expression of forgiveness for unintended errors or mistakes incurred by oneself or by those who work with us in pursuit of a persistent objective, all with good intentions. A sampling of forgiveness stories includes the following considerations:

- **8th Century BC:** Very early during the founding of Rome by Romulus, he and his male followers sought out wives from the surrounding communities. The Sabines were one of those groups and feared the development of a rival society. As a result, the Sabine warriors refused to allow the women from their community to marry the Romans. The Romans, for their part, made a plan to abduct the Sabine women during a festival where they fought off the men. They were then implored by Romulus to accept their Roman husbands. Later, the Sabines planned a counterattack to regain the women. However, in an act of forgiveness, the Sabine women implored the Sabine men not to attack their Roman abductors, who were now their lawfully wedded husbands.

- **April 9, 1865:** The American Civil War was one of the most devastating experiences in the history of the United States of America. It pitted state against state, political groups against one another, family against family, and brother against brother. But, despite all of the pain caused on both sides of the Civil War, Union General Joshua Lawrence Chamberlain gave the ultimate salute of forgiveness when, on the eve of the Confederate surrender at Appomattox, he saluted those same soldiers in a symbol of forgiveness.

- **December 27, 1983:** Pope John Paul II was shot in the abdomen as he passed through St. Peter's Square by Mehmet Ali Agca. But, in an act of forgiveness, the Pontiff forgave him.

***And, like the three examples above, there are many, many more stories
of forgiveness.*** Let me begin by sharing another personal story. This one is
short. I was once asked the question: *"If you could invite 3 or 4 people – either
living or not – to dinner tonight, who would you invite? And, what would you
talk about?"* What a fantastic question. The only problem was that I had to
answer it in the moment...so, in the moment, as I considered the options, my
mind quickly gravitated to three individuals who had made a difference, and I
responded:

> *"Mahatma Gandhi for giving us an approach to resistance that has
> proven to be the most remarkable tool for changing societies, Martin
> Luther King, Jr. for successfully adopting a philosophy that changed the
> direction of a nation as well as setting the stage for recognizing the
> importance of human rights in all societies, Nelson Mandella for
> standing steadfast in his beliefs on behalf of a subjugated people; and,
> Albert Schweitzer, MD as a personal hero for bringing compassionate
> care and resources to those had nothing. Oops! That's four so I would cook
> extra food and learn from all of them. And, we would talk about how to
> make the world a better place and what I needed to do in whatever small
> measure to participate in helping to make the world a better place."*

But, as I considered these four iconic leaders and the example of self-
forgiveness, there was one story that rose to the top as the most compelling –
and that is the story of Nelson Mandela. As I have thought about that
conversation over the many years since the question was first asked of me, the
topic of forgiveness would naturally percolate forward in the conversation on
their contributions to society. As an outsider looking in on their careers and
contributions to society, it would seem that they had to have a heart of
forgiveness along the way. For without such a perspective, their ability to make
the changes they wrought would likely have been less profound.

There are other examples as well, such as the Churchill-Roosevelt dyad, which
withstood the onslaught of Fascism that spread like an infectious virus across
the world during the mid-20th century. Mao Zedong – despite all the negatives

associated with his tenure as the leader of China – lifted the Chinese people to become one of the undisputed leading nations of the 21ˢᵗ century.

But the non-violent opposition to oppression offered by Gandhi, Mandela, and King held strong against the repression of minorities in their respective nations, and through their message of perseverance and persistence, they altered the course of how nations view human rights. Then there was Albert Schweitzer, whose story kept me motivated to get through medical school and always helped me to hold my mission in life to – "make health care better" – as a very real part of my life.

Each of these leaders represents a good starting point for a conversation about forgiveness. However, among them, Nelson Mandela stands out in particular for his efforts to simultaneously engage in forgiveness and release. In my estimation, among the many leaders of the 20ᵗʰ century, he was a premier example of a leader who not only helped to shape the course of human history but also engaged in forgiveness and release.

Forgiveness and release are perhaps the most difficult tasks of any leader. They require strength of character and a clear vision for the future that engages and involves everyone, regardless of their prior role, perspective, or position on the problems facing those working to "make [things] better."

Think about this idea...

Embrace those thoughts...

And, move on to the next page...

True forgiveness of **self** and **others** is a *rare commodity*

too often offered by leaders in a parsimonious fashion.

But when offered...
It captures the hearts and minds of *everyone*
Having the opportunity to work with a persistent leader!

Pause and consider this idea

and then...

Ask yourself the following questions:

What are the areas where you should forgive yourself?

What are the circumstances?

Who on your team deserves the same compassion?

Why should forgiveness be offered?

When can you make restitution?

CHAPTER XVI

The Path Forward

If I cannot do great things,
I can do small things in a great way.

Martin Luther King, Jr.

Finding a guide or mentor is another important consideration for developing effective persistence to support the path forward. Such individuals often offer us unbridled advice and guidance as we grapple with the real and imagined obstacles that line our pathway toward solving a problem or making a difference. I would argue that you should consider finding a reliable mentor rather than a Sherpa-type guide. While the Sherpa can also be valuable, their advice is often specific to their areas of expertise and limited to the portion of the pathway with which they have the most experience.

A reliable mentor, on the other hand, is someone always available at any time to offer advice, consolation, a "whack upside the top of your head"[55], and other forms of advice that are seldom available from others in large measure because they hold a higher degree of intimacy across all aspects of your life. As you walk down the path of serving as a Persistent Leader, a reliable mentor will notice the large rock on the side of the path, the raised speed bump in the middle of the road, the surface disruption up ahead, and the need for slowing down to survive. In most cases, a reliable mentor has been down the road before and can anticipate the obstacles you may face as you move along your path of experience. While your path may be slightly different, the similarities to the mentor's path are often useful guideposts that can be readily used for both their successes and failures.

So, finding a reliable mentor can be an invaluable asset for any Persistent Leader. And how is that accomplished? I think the best route is by simply asking the person who has given you solid advice or guidance if they would be willing to mentor you. Try them out. If it doesn't fit, find a different mentor. Individuals with mentoring credentials will understand the importance of finding the right fit. And, while these senior leaders are generally willing to engage in mentoring, they often have no absolute requirements to engage in mentoring. A reliable mentor is committed to helping the mentee find success and gratification in their chosen professional field. A reliable mentor also empowers the mentee to develop their strengths, beliefs, and personal attributes – to become a reliable Persistent Leader. Finally, a reliable mentor exhibits all of the personal and professional qualities one would expect to find among those who have been successful in their chosen field. In essence, the reliable mentor simply wants to help and share. It's part of the unwritten mentoring code.

In a recent web-based article[56] on mentorship entitled "8 Qualities of a Good Mentor," the essential elements are outlined and bear repeating. They include:

1. A willingness to share skills, knowledge, and expertise that assists the mentee in addressing problems.

2. Demonstrates a positive attitude and acts as a positive role model for the mentee.

3. Takes a personal interest in the mentoring relationship by making themselves available on both a regular and irregular basis.

4. Exhibits enthusiasm in the chosen field of the mentee.

5. Values ongoing learning and growth in the field and assists the mentee by not only engaging with them in these areas but also helping them proactively engage in their field.

6. Provides guidance and constructive feedback both personally and professionally.

7. Is respected by colleagues across the spectrum of people within the organization where they themselves work.

8. Sets and meets ongoing personal and professional goals that can demonstrate to the mentee how persistent leadership works.

Finally, a reliable mentor is someone who is actually involved in the life of their mentee. It's more than just the occasional get-together or sharing. Not only does the mentor affect the life of the mentee, but the mentees, likewise, affect the life of the mentor. You will find, as you go about the process, that the other common characteristic of reliable mentors is that they stand out in the crowd. They have a presence that is palpable, real, and pervasive. As Persistent Leaders themselves, they help people of all stripes sustain and motivate themselves in environments that often are not only unsupportive but can sometimes even be hostile to the ideas, values, and approaches outlined in the preceding chapters as the core elements of a Persistent Leader.

Good luck...and by the way, become *reliable* over time!

CHAPTER XVII

Special Considerations On Persistence With Others

For many problems we face in society, persistence is a long game.
It serves as the framework for involving and working with others.
The big problems we face require more than the energy of one.
Persistence problems of that magnitude require all of us to be
pulling and pushing in the same direction.

Kevin Fickenscher, MD

Although I've highlighted the importance of group persistence, I wanted to close with some final thoughts on the persistence of *working together*. While persistence is a critical aptitude for many aspects of our lives, when adopted in isolation, it is generally reserved for the work we engage in related to our careers, raising a family, developing particular skills, becoming an artist, and other individual endeavors that undoubtedly arise in your thoughts.

Persistence as an individual will help in your pursuit of those individual quests. However, for the problems writ large in society, the engagement of dedicated groups of people is essential. You can lead a group with persistence, but if there are no followers, there is likely to be little progress. Such considerations are especially important for overcoming challenges, maintaining motivation, and achieving shared goals of the committed group. Such a perspective is particularly critical when we are working to establish a corporate culture, to resolve societal problems, or to create a collective movement.

So, what are the types of collective movements I am talking about? Let's consider two notable examples from the last century:[57]

Creating Social Security
During Franklin Roosevelt's Presidency

Roosevelt assumed the Presidency at the height of the Great Depression. Jobs had disappeared, farms were losing their farms, economic stagnation was rampant, and the future for the vast majority of Americans seemed desolate. It was clear to everyone that the Great Depression had devastated families, resulting in widespread poverty and unemployment. One of the hallmark legislative initiatives pursued by the Roosevelt Administration was the mobilization of support for Social Security legislation. But how was this accomplished? Primarily through a combination of public communication, political strategy, coalition-building, and a healthy dose of persistence that included the following key elements:

1. **Framing Social Security as a Response to the Great Depression** – Roosevelt created a public urgency by advocating before Congress, on the radio and before Congress that "Social Security" was a necessary safety net for protecting the elderly, the unemployed, and the disadvantaged from economic insecurity. He framed his argument as the moral obligation of a modern, caring society. It was described as "social insurance, not charity."

2. **Creating the Committee on Economic Security (CES)** – In 1934, Roosevelt established the CES and appointed his Secretary of Labor, Frances Perkins, as its leader. In forming the committee, she brought together notable experts in the fields of economics, social reform, and

public policy to develop legislation with the intent of presenting it to Congress. The composition of the CES clearly created a sense of credibility and due diligence required to gain the support of the people and Congress. They accomplished this objective through their extensive research and a detailed plan, which was presented to Congress in 1935.

3. **Building Support Through Multiple Coalitions** – The entire Administration was mobilized to reach out and work with various labor and progressive groups to create a wave of support for the proposals. They actively pursued support from labor unions, progressive reformers, and social workers who had long advocated for social insurance. They even reached out to the business community, although many of the business leaders opposed government intervention. However, Roosevelt personally engaged them in discussions and emphasized that the plan for Social Security developed by CES would stabilize the economy and maintain the purchasing power among retirees.

4. **Roosevelt Directly Appealed to the Public Through Media** – Roosevelt engaged in the iconic use of the Fireside Chat, which gathered families across the nation around the radio to hear President Roosevelt describe his intent and efforts on their behalf. He also went on public speaking tours where he directly addressed the American people and his Social Security plan in clear terms – again, emphasizing security in old age and protection against poverty. By mobilizing the public in this manner, he placed immeasurable pressure on Congress to act.

5. **Creating a Political Coalition in Congress** – As is common in the US Congress, coalitions are a critical resource for driving successful legislative initiatives toward majority support. Roosevelt and his allies worked strategically within Congress with key Democrats and moderate Republicans to craft a version of the bill that could garner

the support of the majority. The legislation required compromises (e.g., excluding certain job categories, such as domestic and agricultural workers) to ensure legislative approval, only to revisit those modifications at a later date when even more public support had evolved in favor of Social Security. In essence, the strategy was "flexible," "incremental," and "modest." The approach made the bill palatable, with Roosevelt creating the framework for further modifications down the road, which required further persistent work. In fact, Social Security became the cornerstone of the New Deal and one of the most enduring pieces of US social legislation in history for the nation.

In summary, the nuclear disarmament movement was facilitated by a convergence of grassroots activism, humanitarian advocacy, political diplomacy, scientific engagement, and shifting global security dynamics.

...AND...

International Nuclear Disarmament

The nuclear disarmament movement of the last century was shaped and facilitated by a combination of persistent political, social, strategic, and humanitarian factors over time. It is another example of "persistence with others." While it has been disrupted recently, it still stands as one of the major cross-cultural accomplishments of the modern era. So, how did it evolve, and what were the factors that caused it to take hold around the world?

1. **Recognition of Humanitarian Implications** – World War II ended rather precipitously as a result of the devastating consequences of the atomic bomb attacks on Nagasaki and Hiroshima. The shocking pictorial displays on the front pages of newspapers created universal distress throughout the world and precipitated the movement...

2. **Public Awareness and Activism** – The alarming training of school children to sit under desks at school in the event of a nuclear attack created familial hysteria. As a result, "anti-nuclear protests" quickly evolved (e.g., the "Ban the Bomb" in the USA, the Campaign for Nuclear Disarmament in the UK, and other similar movements throughout the world). Action was taken to create the International Campaign to Abolish Nuclear Weapons (ICAN) that mobilized public sentiment worldwide and received the Nobel Peace Prize.

3. **Wide-Spread Publicity on Atomic Accidents and Incidents** – Events such as the Cuban Missile Crisis (1962) and near-launch events due to false alarms (e.g., 1983 Soviet incident)[58] exposed the dangers of maintaining nuclear arsenals.

4. **Political Leadership and Diplomacy** – Over time, the political leadership of multiple different – and, even adversarial – countries came together with common bilateral treaties and agreements, starting in 1968 with the Non-Proliferation Treaty (NPT) as a global framework for preventing nuclear proliferation and encouraging disarmament. Then, the nations moved forward with even stronger

agreements under the leadership of the U.S. and Russia, with the SALT, START, and New START agreements leading to a verifiable reduction, and culminating in the 2017 Treaty on the Prohibition of Nuclear Weapons (TPNW).

5. **Expert Scientific Advocacy and Global Security Planning**– The movement gained momentum [59] from the Reagan-Gorbachev meetings in Iceland and work by the World Affairs Council and the Pugwash Conferences on Science, as well as the support of notable scientists such as Albert Einstein. The potential existential risk and rational calculations of nuclear war were even highlighted by a publication of the Bulletin of the Atomic Scientists – the "Doomsday Clock" – as an alarm bell on the potential for nuclear war.

6. **Humanitarian Impact Conferences**: Solutions were not immediately realized, but the movement gained momentum with events such as the Oslo (2013), Nayarit (2014), and Vienna (2014) accords, which assisted the world's governments in reframing disarmament as a human security issue, not just a strategic one.

7. **Cultural and Media Influence** – In the contemporary world in which we reside, one cannot neglect the impact of traditional and social media as sources for "spreading the word" on a persistent objective. Films such as *Dr. Strangelove* or *The Day After,* along with literature and the plethora of social media postings on the vagaries of nuclear exchange, have assisted in shaping the public perception and concern about the consequences of nuclear war, and the influence of all manner of media in sharing information for wide public consumption.

In essence, for Nuclear Disarmament, the key factors were global recognition of a problem, activation of the public through discourse and information, wide dissemination on the problems associated with fluid access to nuclear capabilities, and the formation of formal groups to articulate policy objectives for the world.

The Essential Elements
For Fostering and Supporting
Successful Persistence Initiatives With Others

These two examples on the preceding pages provide ample evidence of the resources that lie at the disposal of any group committed to a particular persistence objective. While many of the thoughts on individual persistence are apropos of collective persistence, there is a need to highlight certain key differences in the approach toward persistence within this context, including the following considerations:

1. **Clarity of Purpose to Foster and Support a Shared Vision** – When the greater community of citizens and global observers understands and aligns with the common goal, it's easier to stay motivated and push through difficulties.

2. **Create a Sense of Commitment and Accountability** – Pursuing global persistence objectives requires both strong collective as well as personal commitment by groups and individuals to the cause at hand. Such commitment and accountability are sustained through mutual, defined responsibilities where groups are held accountable to one another and the persistent objective.

3. **Communication, Communication and Communication**, or *The Critical C's* – Where active and honest dialogue, discussions, debate, and disagreements are distilled by a culture of listening to foster and support agreements rather than misplaced misunderstanding. Most leaders will recognize that maintaining a rigid adherence to a pre-defined plan that does not accommodate the interests of the involved members of the team leads to frustration and burnout. Therefore, a cultural norm of adaptability and flexibility for meeting the shifting environmental changes of the persistent objective is critical.

4. **Establishing a Culture of Resilience** – However, the pursuit of a persistent objective will inevitably reach a point of resistance from one sector or another. As a leader of persistence, your essential role is to maintain the civility of ensuing dialogue, discussion, debate and disagreements – *The Four Essential D's* for maintaining ongoing persistence. These *4 Essential D's* coupled with the *3 Critical C's* will create an environment of engagement and commitment that extends far beyond any one individual's involvement in the persistent objective. In sum, resilience is the secret sauce of successful initiatives.

5. **Create a Normative Standard of Periodic Celebration** – One of the overlooked requirements for creating energy and support among the core members of the team involved in a persistent objective is periodic celebration. But it should not be reserved only for the biggest of big challenges. Rather, a periodic sidestep into a celebration of even small wins, where learning from mistakes rather than assigning blame, where recognition of individual contributions and recognizing achievement of sub-objectives, or even resetting them, can be shared by the critical participants.

6. **Support Given Begats Reciprocal Support** – When members of the team feel it is safe to bring up new ideas, challenge ongoing approaches, and consider alternatives, they are much more likely to stay engaged. And, engagement over the longer term is an essential underlying objective for creating and sustaining persistence.

7. **Offer Both Intrinsic and Extrinsic Motivation** – Recognition, both individual and group, markers of progress, and periodic rewards for a job well done create the types of incentives that encourage further work toward helping to realize the persistent objective. It's a lesson that has been well-recognized in the corporate world but can easily be adapted for any persistent effort.

Success starts with a first step. Good luck!!

CHAPTER XVIII

A Summary of Lessons Learned

After a great blow, or crisis, after the first shock and then after the nerves have stopped screaming and twitching, you settle down to the new condition of things and feel that all possibility of change has been used up. You adjust yourself, and are sure that the new equilibrium is for eternity. . . But if anything is certain it is that no story is ever over, for the story which we think is over is only a chapter in a story which will not be over, and it isn't the game that is over, it is just an inning, and that game has a lot more than nine innings. When the game stops, it will be called on account of darkness. But it is a long day.

Robert Penn Warren
author of "All the King's Men"

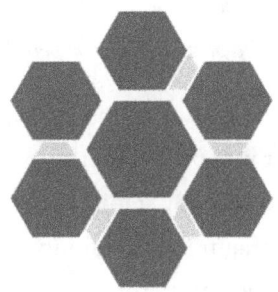

One of my favorite stories was shared with me by a very good friend who is a member of the Navajo Nation. It is a story of leadership and persistence.

Many years ago, when the people were just coming together as a nation, the people were looking for a leader. They looked around and considered all of those who might carry them forward. They turned to the Bear. Over time, they came to a near-universal conclusion that the Bear was not the leader they needed or wanted. The Bear wandered around, often aimlessly, and never seemed to be very focused.

Then, after considering others, the people decided upon the Mountain Lion. But, again, after a short time, they came to realize that despite his bravado and roars, the Mountain Lion was not really leading the people either. He was found most frequently out on the cliffs of the surrounding mountainsides, taking naps. He was never around when his ideas and perspectives were needed by the people. So, they decided he should no longer serve them as their leader.

They then turned to Coyote, who was constantly yelling, howling and chasing others around the land. He made a lot of noise, but the people soon grew tired of his constant whining and whimpering. He did not lead as much as he made lots of noise.

Then, one of the people suggested that instead, they should consider the Mountains. After all, they were there every morning and every evening, looking after the people. So, with a sense of humble admiration, the people turned to the Mountain to serve as their leader. To this day, the Mountain remains a stable presence for the people who look to it every day for leadership and stability.[60]

The one element I have not yet covered on the preceding pages is the concept of *stability*. Leaders need to embody stability for the people they are leading, even in the face of change or failure. And stability emanates from openness and effective communication. Without it, rumors, innuendos, anxieties, and other sidetracks can deflect an organization from effectively pursuing its vision or mission. Stability – even in the face of stormy organizational weather – is an important element for the persistent leader. The seasons in an organization where there are no storms are a rarity. Therefore, stability of presence, stability of mindset, and stability of perspective are crucial characteristics that help an organization sustain itself over the long term. Leaders need to embody this element as if it were their own!

Ultimately, maintaining a persistent journey requires consolidating all the ideas expressed on the preceding pages into a comprehensive macro-strategy. The key lessons of *The Persistence Factor* can be boiled down into the following key considerations:

- Leverage every opportunity and every failure. Savor the moment and learn, learn, learn...
- Embrace all knowledge and accept it when you've distilled the understanding of what the knowledge is imparting to you and your team.
- Be transparent to be effective.
- Culture only changes in increments – unless you're in a revolution – because if you overstep the increments, culture will eat your strategy for lunch every day and spit out the bones.
- Maintain optimism in the face of despair – always.
- Look at yourself first rather than blaming others, and always maintain your humility in all situations.
- Embrace the emptiness of failure and fill yourself with understanding.
- Nurture the seeds of success tenderly and prune where necessary.
- The moment is the moment. The future is a lifetime of moments. So, embrace every moment but seize the future.
- Faith is internal, so always keep your flame lit and watch over it carefully.
- Never trust a person who always says "yes" without question.
- Listen to everyone, especially those who care about you for who you are, not for what you could be.
- Always reflect on your persistent path in silence with yourself and choose wisely.
- Be humble.

Key Lessons From The Persistence Factor – This book intends to provide you with a foundation for accomplishing the mission, goals, and objectives you set for yourself, not simply a project, but as the basis for living your life and contributing to society. Persistence is the factor that supports meaningful and lasting change. It is also an important starting point for changing you. By adopting a persistent approach to life, you can change your network. Your profession, and the world. So, what are the key lessons to put in your pocket and consider every day? They include the following:

1. **Adopting the Persistence Cycle** – Persistence requires continuous work on the cycle of Purpose, Consider, Commit, Focus, Assess, Integrate...to Persist and then, Repeat – over and over and over again...

2. **Consistency in Your Approach to Change** – Change that makes a difference and improves the situation or lives around you requires consistent effort. By using the *Persistence Cycle,* you will be able to effectively adopt goals and objectives that will drive success not only for you but also for those around you.

3. **Developing Expertise Over Time Is Essential** – As with short-term projects or initiatives, a certain degree of learning occurs to help you meet similar challenges in the future. Expertise is the outcome of persistent effort and requires a commitment to learning, sometimes repeatedly.

4. **Adaptability** – Recognizing that change is dynamic, where new situations and challenges continually emerge, fosters a collaborative environment where strategies can be adjusted, situational learning is the norm, and lessons learned are integrated. This enables change in the right direction to be achieved.

5. **Vision – But Not Near-Sighted Vision** – Many leaders strive to hold a vision, but change requires adopting a long-term perspective on achieving the goals of that vision. While short-term results are

important, maintaining a focus on the long-term goals by offering a vision requires persistent *nudging*.

6. **Facing Failure** – One of the natural outcomes of any persistent objective is failure. However, through failure, we can learn to improve, to adapt, and to alter our course, continuing down the road with the energy of the Persistence Factor.

7. **Celebrating Success** – When successes occur, even minor ones, it is essential to offer a celebration that focuses on those who contributed to making the success a reality. But, then you need to *integrate* the successes into the ongoing change effort.

8. **Don't Desire, But Rather Inspire** – Persistent individuals naturally tend to percolate to the top as leaders and role models through their influence on the requisite change needed for solving and meeting long-term challenges. Developing the requisite skills for serving as an inspirational leader is more than just talk. It requires the ability to gather the strength of the followers who help you make persistence real.

9. **Cultivate Patience In Self And Among Followers** – Long-term change requires patience – the synonym for persistence! Sustainable change rarely occurs in the short term. Patience, therefore, is the virtue that complements persistence in the journey of change you inspire with others.

10. **Accepting When It's Time to Redirect** – The one element that has received little attention on the preceding pages is the notion of redirecting or setting aside the focus of your persistent efforts or the persistent objective. For some initiatives, there comes a time when it is important to reconsider your objectives and potentially set your efforts aside or redirect your energies towards other initiatives. This does not mean that you "give up" on it, but it does mean that you intentionally put it aside for another day.

Such a decision is often very difficult, but it is also a very important step in the evolution of persistence. If you are solo, it's your decision. However, if it is being pursued with others on a team of committed individuals working on the persistent objective, it will require dialogue, discussion and debate. Do you need to continue? Should you redirect your individual and/or group efforts toward yet a different direction with the same goal in mind? Or, should you and the other committed members of your team simply discontinue your efforts? These are difficult decisions and require reflection, not as an individual but with those who have invested their trust and energy toward the persistent objective at hand. If you decide to proceed...

Now is the time...
To use these ideas – plus your own –
to create a personal list that you review every day
to maintain your focus and help you stay on course
with your persistent objective by:
Confirming your commitment and direction,
Posting that commitment and direction where you will see it every
morning...
Defining the tasks at hand...
Sharing them...
Debating and considering them...
Revising them – as needed – over time...
And, then...

Adopting and Engaging

The

PERSISTENCE

Factor

A Final Thought – The world is changing at a pace never before experienced in the history of mankind. That's a strong statement, but there are many indicators on the horizon suggesting the comment is on target. If we thought the Enlightenment (c. 1680 – 1800), the Industrial Revolution (c. 1760 – 1840), the Era of the Two World Wars (c. 1914 – 1945+), or the Cultural Revolution (c. 1960 – 1980) represented periods of rapid change, I predict those eras will not be able to hold a candle to the changes that will emanate over the coming decades. The pace of change we are experiencing now is dramatically accelerating beyond each of those prior societal experiences and will require the persistent adoption of changes emerging on the horizon of our global society.

In such an environment, it seems evident that those who can successfully embrace change will serve as the ultimate contributors to the global society as a whole. In many respects, embracing change appears to be the hallmark of successful societies worldwide. Just as we have moved from traveling hunters and gatherers to living and working in small communities to residing in nation-states, we will soon be entering the era of the interconnected global society. Our boundaries are shifting with the globalization of the human community, requiring a persistent focus on how to facilitate effective change.

As such, there is a need for all of us to learn and embrace the art of change outlined in the previous pages of *The Persistence Factor*. Use it as a resource for facilitating effective change. Such an embrace will help all of us to reach new potential and continue our path toward learnings that facilitate the improvement of the human condition.

Good Luck!

Stories of Persistence

In the end, we'll all become stories.

Margaret Atwood

There are many stories of people who've overcome difficulties and exemplify the critical characteristics and essential elements of persistent leadership. The following represents a small sample of notable individuals we all admire for their accomplishments in life. Their life lessons often serve as better examples of persistence than the longer explanations and outlines of essential elements. They are offered as a resource for those looking for good examples.

Abraham Lincoln – There is probably no better example of failure and persistence in the history of American leaders. Let me share Lincoln's life history with you. First, he was a man born into poverty in a one-room cabin in the State of Illinois, and he faced defeat multiple times throughout his life. In many ways, Lincoln epitomizes the concept of persistence.

- His family lost their one-room cabin when Lincoln was a mere 7-year-old child.
- He then lost his mother at age 9.
- He failed in business at the age of 21.

- He was defeated in his first legislative race at age 22.
- He failed yet again in a second business venture at age 24.
- He overcame the death of his sweetheart to whom he was betrothed at age 26.
- He had a nervous breakdown at age 27.
- He lost a congressional race at age 34.
- He sought a job as the land officer for the state of Illinois and was rejected at age 35.
- He then lost a senatorial race at age 45
- He failed in his bid to become the Vice-President nominee by garnering less than 100 votes at age 47.
- He lost a second senatorial race at age 49.
- And, finally, he was elected President of the United States at age 52.

Would you dare call him a failure? He could have quit at any point along the way. But to Lincoln, defeat was a detour and not a dead end. It was a great source of learning. He represents the essence of persistence.

Sir Ernest Henry Shackleton – Ever since I first heard the story of the *Endurance*, I've been intrigued by Shackleton. He lived during the Heroic Age of Antarctic Exploration, which spanned the turn of the last century, around 1900. It was during this period that many explorers tried their best to reach the *South Pole*. When Shackleton missed his chance because another explorer (Roald Amundsen) altered his quest and, instead, turned his attention to crossing Antarctica from sea to sea via travel through the pole. Unfortunately, rather than success, he experienced a crushing defeat when disaster struck his expedition with his ship, Endurance, becoming trapped in the ice where the glaciers of Antarctica slowly crushed it. Following the venture of 1917, he tried one more time in 1921 – only to die from a heart attack while his ship was moored in South Georgia. So, why is he a leader of repute? It's largely because, in the face of insurmountable odds, Shackleton's leadership kept his team together. They didn't fall apart. While the environment subdued their ship, it did not subdue them.

Sir Edmund Hillary – He was the first man – in the known world – to successfully climb Mount Everest. It happened on May 29, 1953, when word spread across the globe that Hillary had scaled the highest mountain then known to man, at 29,032 feet, straight up. For his efforts in scaling the mountain, he was knighted by Queen Elizabeth II. He went on to achieve some degree of international notoriety, even appearing in American Express card commercials because of it! What most people did not know at the time was the degree of failure and missteps that had occurred in his quest before his success. In his book, *High Adventure*, Hillary describes his sense of failure in his quest before the final successful ascent. Why? In 1952, he had previously attempted to climb Mount Everest but failed. Following that quest, when he returned to England, a group asked him to address their members. As he walked on stage, there was thunderous applause as recognition for his attempt at greatness. However, Edmund Hillary did not feel any of it. He saw himself as a failure. As the applause died down, he moved away from the microphone and walked to the edge of the platform. He stood before the audience, made a fist, and pointed at a picture of the mountain. With a very loud voice, he shouted out: "Mount Everest, you beat me the first time, but I'll beat you the next time because you've grown all you are going to grow... but I'm still growing!" This is the essence of persistence – the continuous, chronic, repeating growth that occurs as we work to improve.

Walt Disney – If there is an example of a successful businessperson, artist, or creator, it is Walt Disney. His formal education ended in the eighth grade, and even that formal element of his learning was interrupted regularly. Some scholars have pointed to the fact that Disney suffered from attention deficit hyperactivity disorder (ADHD) as the reason for his problems in the early years. However, there's no real evidence to support this claim. More likely, it is simply because of the environment in which he grew up, where he was continually working for his father. Despite his lack of formal education, he was not dismayed, and he never stopped learning. Throughout his entire life, he read, taught himself, and learned animation; he tried new ways of solving artistic problems and worked tirelessly to improve his craft. And, most importantly, he came to understand his limitations. He is quoted as saying: "All you've got to do is own up to your ignorance honestly, and you'll find people who are eager to fill your head with information." Then, he went a step further and said, "Do a good job. You don't have to worry about the money; it will take care of itself. Just do your best work — then try to trump it." And then on the lessons from failing or being persistent, he said, "I failed... I think it's important to have a good, hard failure when you're young... I learned a lot from that...All the adversity I've had in my life, all my troubles and obstacles, have strengthened me. ... You may not realize it when it happens, but a kick in the teeth may be the best thing in the world for you."

Terrance Stanley Fox – The story of Terry Fox and his journey is ubiquitous among Canadians. He is known for inspiring a nation and offering hope to those who have suffered the ravages of cancer. Terry was born on the Central Plains in Winnipeg, Manitoba, on July 28, 1958. He grew up in Port Coquitlam, British Columbia, where at the age of 18, he was unfortunately diagnosed with Osteogenic Sarcoma – a type of bone cancer that is highly malignant. Terry lost his right leg to cancer. During the course of his treatment, he witnessed the ravages of cancer suffered by so many others, often younger than his own young years. It etched in his mind the suffering of other cancer victims to such a point that he determined he would not leave this "world of miracles" before a cure had been found. So, he developed an audacious plan to raise funds by running the length of Canada. He planned a 5,300-mile run, covering 26 miles a day (or 42 kilometers). He first dipped his foot in the Atlantic on April 12, 1980, at St. John's, Newfoundland. He then began a daily press across the nation by essentially running a marathon a day! He was able to reach Ontario in June of that year, but when he reached the goal at mile 3,339 (5,373 kilometers) after 143 days of continuous running, the recurring cancer forced him to seek further cancer care. The primary bone cancer had metastasized to his lungs, and he could no longer run the distance. In speaking to the people of Ontario, he said: *"Dreams are made if people only try. I believe in miracles...I have to...because somewhere the hurting must stop."* He offered that challenge to the Canadians as a point of inspiration, due to his perseverance in facing overwhelming odds and continuing his quest by contributing to ongoing efforts to raise funds for cancer research. He set a goal of raising $1 for every Canadian alive at the time, or approximately 24 million people. As of mid-year 2024, over $850 million had been raised for cancer research as a tribute to one person showing persistence and resolve. While the Marathon of Hope came to an end, the strength, commitment, and determination of the Canadian people have continued.

J.K. Rowling – J.K. Rowling, the author of the *Harry Potter* series of novels, had a considerable amount of discouragement before hitting the big time. In the early years, she worked as a waitress and, at one point, received public assistance while writing the first installment of the infamous series. The *Harry Potter* book series would go on to become one of the best-selling in modern history, with translations into more than 80 languages, after experiencing rejection by a dozen publishers. The only reason it was finally published is that the eight-year-old daughter of the CEO of Bloomsbury Publishers begged him to publish it. She thought the book was great! And, it was... Rowling has faced many points of failure throughout her life, but has always held the notion of "persistence" as a cornerstone for moving forward. She has noted that: *"Failure meant a stripping away of the inessential."* Indeed. Failure helps us to focus and consider the nubbin that will make a difference both in our life...on a project...in making a difference. In life, there are often setbacks, roadblocks, and obstacles that obstruct our way forward. But the focus and persistence, those setbacks, roadblocks, and obstacles, can be removed and mitigated through persistence.

Malala Yousafzai – In 2009, when the Taliban took control of her homeland in Pakistan and decreed that educating girls would soon be a crime, a 12-year-old girl attending a school under Taliban control used a pseudonym and began writing for the BBC blog. She felt that girls deserved education, and she wanted to share her own plight. Malala wrote about topics ranging from her desire to become a doctor to her fear that her school would be targeted and attacked. For the first time, people outside Pakistan were experiencing a vulnerable, first-person account of Taliban rule from the perspective of a young girl who was living it. When journalists with the *New York Times* heard about her story, they contacted Malala to request an interview. Because the family felt it was important for Malala's message to reach a broader audience that might understand the plight of girls seeking education, they agreed. But the leaders of the Taliban were enraged. The subsequent turn of events was ugly. In the days following the award of the Pakistan National Youth Peace Prize to Malala for advocating in support of girls' education, a group of Taliban soldiers boarded the school bus she was riding on the way to school and shot her in the head and neck. She was immediately rushed to the hospital, and then airlifted to safety in the United Kingdom, where she miraculously lived! But that didn't stop Malala. She was persistent. Despite the near-death experience, she continued her advocacy. It strengthened her resolve, and she extended her message when more than 2 million Pakistani people signed a petition on the *Right to Education Bill,* culminating in the adoption of the *Right to Free and Compulsory Education Bill* by the national legislature. Due in large measure to Malala's persistence, she was awarded the Nobel Peace Prize in 2014. Persistence is about stiffened resolve if, in your heart, you know you're right.

Apostle Paul – There are many examples of religious leaders exemplifying acts of persistence in the face of tremendous persecution or toil. It seems clear that without the conversion of the Apostle Paul to the teaching of Jesus, the entire foundation of Christianity would likely be missing from society. My father-in-law, an academic theologian and author of numerous books, many of which focus on the Apostle Paul, noted in his writing that the Apostle Paul was a true "messenger" for carrying the words of Jesus forward. The word "Apostle" is derived from the Greek word Apostolos, meaning "the one who is sent." Paul derived his sense of mission from his clear calling or sense of direction regarding his role in spreading the Word of Jesus throughout the Middle East and Asia. He believed! So, he had a calling to perform in the manner that Jesus outlined for him in Acts, Verse 9: "*...Saul (who changed his name to become Paul) is a chosen instrument of Mine, to bear My name before* *the Gentiles and kings and the sons of Israel."* He even endured persecution by Rome until the conversion of the empire in 313 AD, when Emperor Constantine issued the Edict of Milan, accepting Christianity, which became the state religion ten years later. Even though there was some distance between the time of Paul and the issuance of the edict, it occurred in large measure because of the groundwork laid by the Apostle Paul in spreading the Word. The same argument can be made for other religious or spiritual leaders as follows.

Rumi – offered many thoughts on the notion of persistence. The following quotes are examples of his thoughts on the topic:

- "...keep knocking and the joy inside will eventually open a window and look out to see who's there".

- "Whatever happens to you, don't fall into despair. Even if all the doors are closed, a secret path will be there for you that no one knows. You can't see it yet, but so many paradises are at the end of this path. Be grateful. It is easy to thank after obtaining what you want. Thank before having what you want."

- "I said: What about my eyes?
  He said: Keep them on the road.
  I said: What about my passion?
  He said: Keep it burning.
  I said: What about my heart?
  He said: Tell me what you hold inside it?
  I said: Pain and sorrow.
  He said: Stay with it.
  The wound is the place where the Light enters you."

Buddha – Another example of conversion that created a sense of persistence leading toward the creation of a new religious mode is Buddha. He combined the concept of persistence with both focus, concentration and mindfulness as the mode for making change happen in the world. In fact, the charge to the monks who followed the teachings of Buddha included a focus on five "faculties", including the faculty of conviction, the faculty of persistence, the faculty of mindfulness, the faculty of concentration, and the faculty of discernment. As conveyed by Buddha, accepting, embracing, and developing these five faculties was an essential element for becoming a monk. Rather than describe his thoughts, here is a direct quote from Buddha on the topic of persistence:

> *"There's the case where a monk, a disciple of the noble ones, keeps his persistence aroused for abandoning unskillful mental qualities and taking on skillful mental qualities. He is steadfast, solid in his effort, not shirking his duties with regard to skillful mental qualities. He generates desire, endeavors, arouses persistence, upholds and exerts his intent for the sake of the non-arising of evil, unskillful qualities that have not yet arisen... for the sake of the abandoning of evil, unskillful qualities that have arisen... for the sake of the arising of skillful qualities that have not yet arisen... (and) for the maintenance, non-confusion, increase, plenitude, development, and culmination of skillful qualities that have arisen."*

It's important to remember these connections among persistence, mindfulness, and concentration. All too often, they are forgotten, leading to many different misunderstandings about what mindfulness and concentration are.

The Successful Alcoholic – One of the most difficult tasks that any addicted person can take on is to become unaddicted. While treatment is an essential component of the overall treatment plan, lasting sobriety relies on what is commonly referred to as, *The Five P's of Successful Recovery*. Sobriety can start with treatment where the focus is on care, support, planning, and other essential activities designed to help the addicted individual move back into society. However, sobriety is sustained by these five essential areas of focus, including:

1. **Purpose**. A sense of purpose is the foundation for successful recovery. It can include the pursuit of a dream, a desired accomplishment that holds meaning, or a deeply held goal. Regardless of the source, the purpose is to generate the strength and energy that we use to sustain our daily activities. And, without purpose, setting a direction, accepting a challenge, or engaging with others is difficult to sustain. For myself, I not only carry a copy of my "Seven Essentials," but they are also posted on the mirror in my bathroom so that when I get up in the morning, it is the first message I see – right there in front of me on the mirror so that I can't miss it.

2. **Practice.** In seeking recovery, change is an absolute requirement – of our responses to daily events, to the way we process information, to our management of the internal stresses that invariably affect our interactions with others. The practice has been likened to the skills we require for learning to play an instrument, singing (on key, of course), painting a picture, or developing a new skill. We essentially need to "practice" to gain the essential behaviors and skills required for successful work with others.

3. **Perseverance or Persistence.** It is a rare task or activity that is accomplished in a short period. Like sobriety, it takes time, focus, and initiative to be successful or, as many counselors will tell you, "it's not a sprint...it's a marathon that can take time. In fact, like the addicted personality, success on an initiative or project can take a lifetime of effort to see the final results. Persistence is the name of the game.

4. **Pray or Pause**. If prayer isn't for you, try contemplation, where you set aside time out of every day to reflect, consider, digest, ponder, reflect, and deliberate on the world around you and your place in it. For most of us, we need a sense of something greater than ourselves as a source of strength and vision that gives us the drive to get up and do the things that need to be done in our lives. The daily prayer or pause (take your preference) is one way of accomplishing that objective.

5. **Praise.** Too often in life, we focus on the negative. What have we done wrong? What problems were created? But, embedded in our trials and tribulations are the essential elements of learning about the good and contributory elements we've offered to projects, or, simply, ourselves. Taking a moment to offer ourselves a bit of praise through personal acceptance of gratitude is an important part of the mantras we need to create in our lives.

Me, Myself and I – On my 65th birthday (February 23, 2015), I received the following dispatch from my close friend and colleague, Bobby T. It was the astrology reading for that date about PISCES (Feb. 19-March 20). It read:

> *The British rock band The Animals released their gritty, growly song "The House of the Rising Sun" in 1964. It reached the top of the pop music charts in the U.S., Canada, the U.K., and Australia, and was a hit with critics. *Rolling Stone* magazine ultimately ranked it as the 122nd greatest song of all time. And yet it took the Animals just 15 minutes to record. They did it in one take. That's the kind of beginner's luck and spontaneous flow I foresee you having in the coming weeks, Pisces. What's the best way for you to channel all that soulful mojo?*

My friend had several recommended modifications I could make in my leadership style, but the essence was that as a leader of change, I needed to be "persistent".

While some would argue I was finally over the proverbial hill at that age, I realized on that wonderful, extremely cold, snowy day in Maine that I didn't feel *"...over the hill"*. On that day, I gazed out the windows of my home overlooking a bay off the Atlantic Ocean and wrote down in my diary that life was *"...not so bad once you're over the hill. You find that there are simply more hills, except for that huge mountain off on the horizon that seems dark and foreboding with lightning and clouds surrounding it. That mountain seems a bit ominous, but the rest of those hills are simply that – hills... And, besides, the mountain is (hopefully) a long way off."*

Not a bad perspective for maintaining persistence. Then, I received a note from that same friend who forwarded his local newspaper citation on *PISCES (Feb. 19-March 20)* for that date. *It stated: "What would your best mother do in a situation like this? Please note that I'm not asking: What would your mother do? I'm not suggesting you call on the counsel of your actual mother. When I use the term "your best mother," I'm referring to the archetype of your perfect mother. Imagine a wise older woman who understands you telepathically, loves you unconditionally, and wants you to live your life according to your own inner necessity, not hers or anyone else's. Visualize her. Call on her. Seek her blessings."*

Again, persistence...it's the name of the game! Hopefully, the thoughts, perspectives, and approaches to persistence described in this book will serve a useful purpose for you. And, as a final note and as you turn the page, I recommend that you memorize the first quote in Appendix B under "Purpose". It's a great way to think about how you can embrace your personal persistence!

Quotes For Adoption and Assistance In the Journey of Your Choosing

Purpose

Starting with your purpose is the most important first step. These are the most resonant quotes about finding one's purpose that I've collected over the years, spanning wisdom, creativity, struggle, and soul-searching from thought leaders, artists, and change-makers who lived the question deeply...

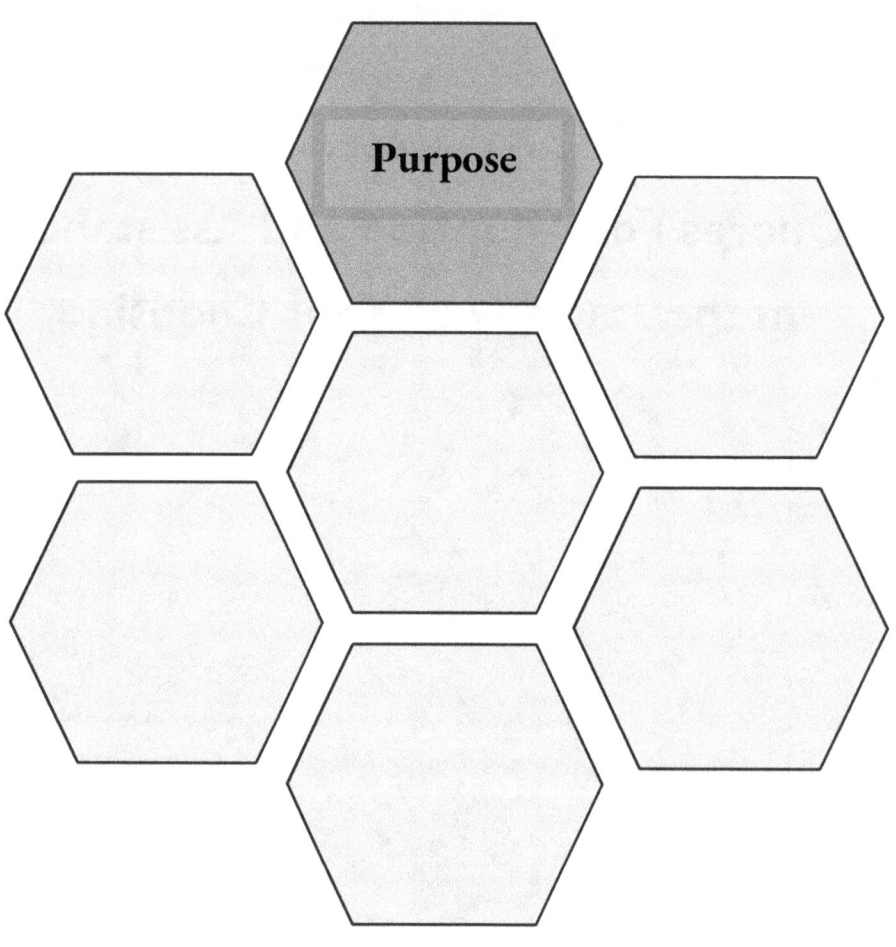

A dream is a wish your heart makes, when you're fast asleep. In dreams you have your heartaches, the dreams you wish for and keep. Have faith in your dreams and someday, your dreams will come shining through. For if you keep on believing, the dreams you wish for come true.

Mickey Mouse
The author's favorite quote of all time...

The two most important days in your life are the day you are born and the day you find out why.
AND
The two most important days in your life are the day you are born and the day you find out why.

Mark Twain
Timeless quotes that capture the moment
purpose clicks into clarity

Your purpose in life is to find your purpose and give your whole heart and soul to it.

Buddha (attributed)
Purpose as a devotion, not just a destination

Don't ask what the world needs. Ask what makes you come alive, and go do it. Because what the world needs is people who have come alive.

Howard Thurman
A deep call to align inner fire with outer need

When you find your path, you must not be afraid. You need to have sufficient courage to make mistakes.

Paulo Coelho
Purpose isn't about being perfect—
it's about being brave enough to keep walking.

We are not here merely to make a living. We are here to enrich the world.

Woodrow Wilson

Purpose is bigger than personal success—it's about contribution.

Purpose is the place where your deep gladness meets the world's deep need.

Frederick Buechner

A beautiful intersection of passion and service

Efforts and courage are not enough without purpose and direction.

John F. Kennedy

Even boldness needs a compass.

The meaning of life is to find your gift. The purpose of life is to give it away.

Pablo Picasso (attributed)

Art meets generosity—purpose as a gift in motion

He who has a why to live can bear almost any how.

Friedrich Nietzsche

A profound truth echoed later by Viktor Frankl: purpose is the fuel of survival.

In a real sense, all life is interrelated. All...are caught in an inescapable network of mutuality, tied in a single garment of destiny.

Martin Luther King, Jr.

The greatest oak was once a little nut who held its ground.

Anonymous

Live as if you were to die tomorrow. Learn as if you were to live forever.

Mahatma Gandhi

The secret of success is constancy to purpose.

Benjamin Disraeli

People of mediocre ability sometimes achieve outstanding success because they don't know when to quit. Most men succeed because they are determined to.

George Allen

I am of the opinion that my life belongs to the community, and as long as I live, it is my privilege to do for it whatever I can.

George Bernard Shaw

We make a living by what we get, but we make a life by what we give.

Sir Winston Churchill

All of us invent ourselves. Some of us just have more imagination than others.

Cher

I believe purpose is something we build, not something we find.

Mel Robbins

For those who feel unsure: purpose can be made, not just discovered.

Remembering that I'll be dead soon is the most important tool I've ever encountered to help me make the big choices in life. Because almost everything - all external expectations, all pride, all fear of embarrassment or failure - these things just fall away in the face of death, leaving only what is truly important.

Steve Jobs

One of the core goals of life is survival; the other is meaning.

Sebastian Junger

Live the life you've always dreamed of. Be fearless in the face of adversity. Never stop learning. Use your imagination whenever possible. Recognize the beauty that surrounds you. Remember where you came from, but never lose sight of where you are going.

Frequently attributed to Les Brown
A motivational speaker who is frequently cited as
the source of the statement, although
the quote is derived from an Unknown Source

There are people who have developed a particular antipathy toward the search for knowledge, whose inner doors are fastened tight against anything that might cast doubt on what they believe they already know. Why seek truth if truth will require us to do the hard work of rethinking? ...So as we shake our heads at those charmed by charlatans and demagogues, let us not exempt ourselves."

Mark Lilla

To be yourself in a world that is constantly trying to make you something else is the greatest accomplishment.

Ralph Waldo Emerson

Consideration

The importance of CONSIDERATION cannot be overstated. Choosing *what* to do in life, leadership, or change work isn't just about action – it's about how you think, reflect, and weigh your choices. These quotes offer deep wisdom on how to consider your path, your priorities, and your impact...

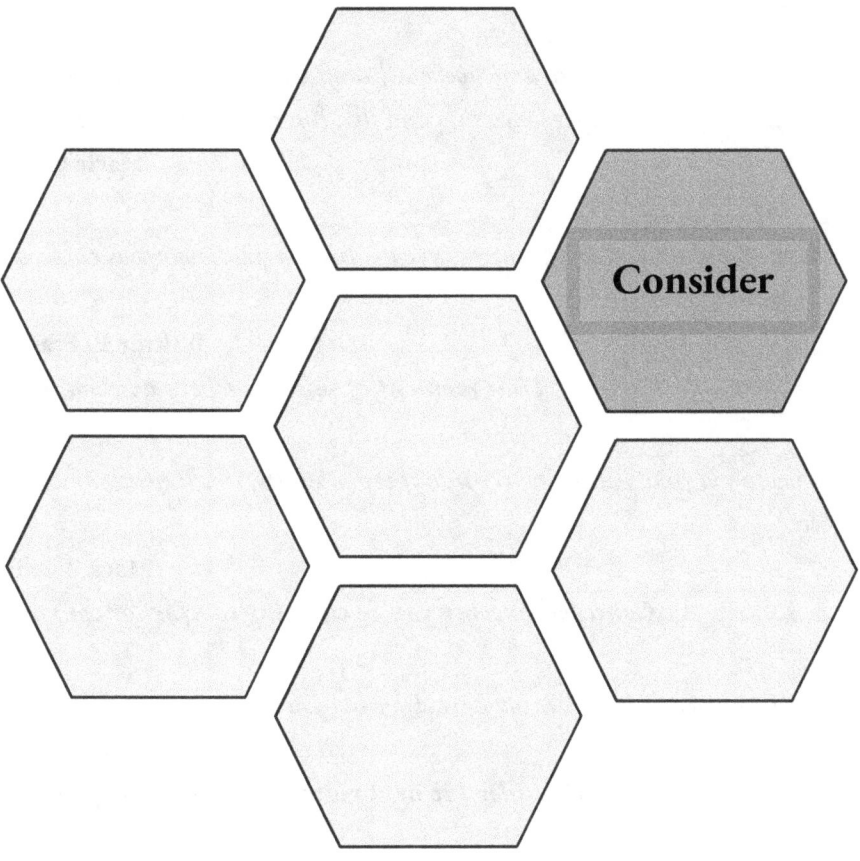

In the middle of every difficulty lies opportunity.

Aıbert Einstein
Consider what's possible, not just what's hard

It is not enough to be busy. So are the ants. The question is: What are we busy about?

Henry David Thoreau
Activity isn't purpose—alignment is

We must have perseverance and above all confidence in ourselves. We must believe that we are gifted for something and that this thing must be attained.

Marie Curie

Between stimulus and response there is a space. In that space is our power to choose our response.

Viktor E. Frankı
That moment of pause is where wisdom lives.

Whenever you find yourself on the side of the majority, it is time to pause and reflect.

Mark Twain
Consider whether you're choosing comfort or courage.

Start where you are. Use what you have. Do what you can.

Arthur Ashe
Consider the next right step, not the perfect one.

If you don't prioritize your life, someone else will.

Greg McKeown, Essentiaıism
Consider who's steering your choices—you or others?

Am I doing this out of love, or out of fear?

Eiisabeth Kübier-Ross (paraphrased)
A powerful inner filter when facing big decisions

Don't be pushed around by the fears in your mind. Be led by the dreams in your heart.

Roy T. Bennett
Consider whether fear or vision is driving the bus

Clarity comes from engagement, not thought.

Marie Forieo
Sometimes, you consider by doing, not overthinking

What you do makes a difference, and you have to decide what kind of difference you want to make.

Jane Goodaii
A powerful way to frame your decisions: impact over image

Between stimulus and response there is a space. In that space is our power to choose our response.

Viktor E. Franki
That moment of pause is where wisdom lives.

Problems are only opportunity in work clothes.

Henry J. Kaiser
Shipbuilding Titan

It's fine to celebrate success but it is more important to heed the lessons of failure.

Biii Gates
Founder, Microsoft

Ever since I was a little girl, I always wanted to be somebody. Now I see I should have been more specific.

Lily Tomlin

Failing to seize opportunities. It's the worst kind of failure.

Ian Kazi Shakil
Cofounder of Augmedix

Let us put our minds together and see what life can make for our children.

Sitting Bull
Hunkpapa Lakota Sioux leader

When did the future switch from being a promise to being a threat?"

Chuck Palahniuk
Novelist, The Knowledge

Commitment

COMMITMENT is where purpose gets teeth. It's what turns vision into action, and action into transformation, and transformation into reality. Here is a set of quotes on *developing a deep, durable sense of commitment* to something that matters...

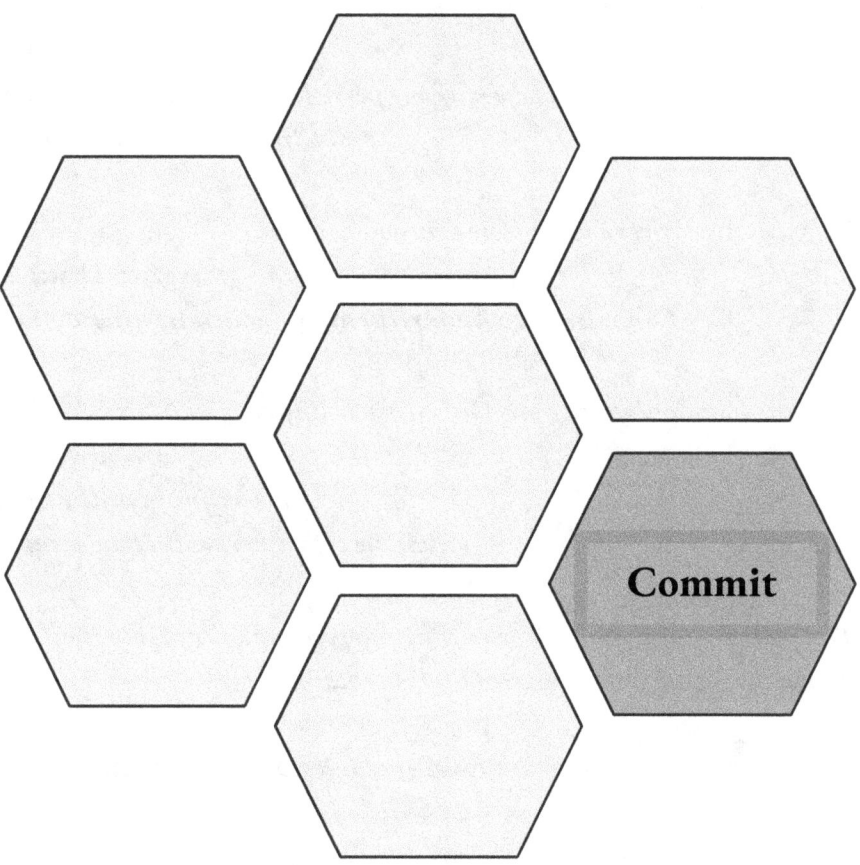

Commit

Unless commitment is made, there are only promises and hopes;
but no plans.

Peter F. Drucker
Commitment is the line between wishing and working.

Commitment means staying loyal to what you said you were going to do long
after the mood you said it in has left you.

Unknown
Purpose without persistence is a feeling and with
commitment, it becomes a force.

You may have to fight a battle more than once to win it.

Margaret Thatcher
Commitment means returning—especially after defeat.

Without commitment, you cannot have depth in anything.

Neil Strauss
Depth requires dedication.
Shallow effort brings shallow results.

The quality of a person's life is in direct proportion to their commitment to
excellence, regardless of their chosen field of endeavor.

Vince Lombardi
Excellence is a byproduct of being all in.

There are only two options regarding commitment. You're either in or you're out.
There's no such thing as life in-between.

Pat Riley
Commitment asks for clarity, not half-measures

The moment one definitely commits oneself, then Providence moves too.

W.H. Murray

Courage is the commitment to begin without any guarantee of success.

Johann Woifgang von Goethe (attributed)

Purpose-driven commitment doesn't wait for certainty

Act as if what you do makes a difference. It does.

Wiiiiam James

This belief fuels commitment—it keeps you moving even when results aren't immediate.

Never follow a Leader who is more in love with power than People.

Native American Indian Proverb

Freedom is not the absence of commitments, but the ability to choose—and commit myself to—what is best for me.

Pauio Coeiho

Commitment isn't a cage—it's an act of empowered choice

Come, come, whoever you are. Wanderer, worshiper, lover of leaving. It doesn't matter. Ours is not a caravan of despair. Come, even if you have broken your vows a thousand times. Come, yet again. Come, come.

Jaiaiuddin Rumi

Our greatest glory is not in never failing, but in rising up every time we fail.

Raiph Waido Emerson

Not everything that is faced can be change, but nothing can be changed until it is faced.

James Baidwin

He conquers who endures.

Persius

Most people never run far enough on their first wind to find out they've got a second.

William James

No great thing is created suddenly.

Epictetus

I can accept failure, everyone fails at something. But I can't accept not trying.
Michael Jordan

Success is no accident. It is hard work, perseverance, learning, studying, sacrifice and, most of all, love of what you are doing or learning to do.

Pele
Considered one of the premier soccer players in the history of the sport

Failures, repeated failures, are finger posts on the road to achievement. One fails forward toward success.

C. S. Lewis

An essential aspect of creativity is not being afraid to fail.

Edwin Land
Inventor of the Polaroid camera to satisfy his daughter's need for "immediate" pictures

A failure is not always a mistake; it may simply be the best one can do under the circumstances. The real mistake is to stop trying.

B. F. Skinner

Far better is it to dare mighty things, to win glorious triumphs, even though checkered by failure...than to rank with those poor spirits who neither enjoy nor suffer much, because they live in a gray twilight that knows not victory nor defeat.

Theodore Roosevelt
26th President of the United States

It is impossible to live without failing at something, unless you live so cautiously that you might as well not have lived at all, in which case you have failed by default.

J. K. Rowling

I don't think of myself as a poor deprived ghetto girl who made good. I think of myself as somebody who from an early age knew I was responsible for myself, and I had to make good.

Oprah Winfrey
She persisted by not dwelling on her upbringing, which was filled with abuse and abject poverty

When the power of Love overcomes the love of power, the world will know peace.

Jimi Hendrix

Progress is impossible without change, and those who cannot change their minds cannot change anything.

George Bernard Shaw

Impossible is just a big word thrown around by small men who find it easier to live in the world they've been given than to explore the power they have to change it. Impossible is not a fact. It's an opinion. It's not a declaration. It's a dare. Impossible is potential. Impossible is temporary. Impossible is nothing.

Muhammad Ali
On the importance of self-belief, conviction, and the importance of fighting for a cause, even when facing opposition.

Don't bend; don't water it down; don't try to make it logical; don't edit your own soul according to fashion. Rather, follow your most intense obsessions mercilessly.

Anne Rice

Dreams are made if people only try. I believe in miracles...I have to...because somewhere the hurting must stop.

Terrance Stanley Fox

He inspired Canada with his Marathon of Hope, a cross-Canada run that not only raised $24 million for cancer research but also inspired an entire generation of Canadians through his determination and devotion.

I used to think the point was to learn a piece and play it perfectly. But then it occurred to me that isn't the point. The point is to learn what the piece wants to teach me.

Karen Yancy Dodson

Stimulating solutions in society as a musician and activist

When we started University Games my cofounder and I said we have three goals: always be profitable, maintain our friendship, and have fun every day. We haven't succeeded in having fun every day. Other than that I don't think about failure. I'm always redefining success.

Bob Moog

CEO, University Games

Knowing one's commitment is an essential foundation for understanding one's pursuit of persistence.

AND

Persistence is about doing what's right and should be done!

Kevin Fickenscher

Author, The Persistence Factor

Focus

FOCUS is what keeps persistence from turning into burnout. It's the discipline of saying *no* to distractions so you can say *yes* to what really matters. Here are a few powerful quotes on the need for *focus* in the journey of persistence...

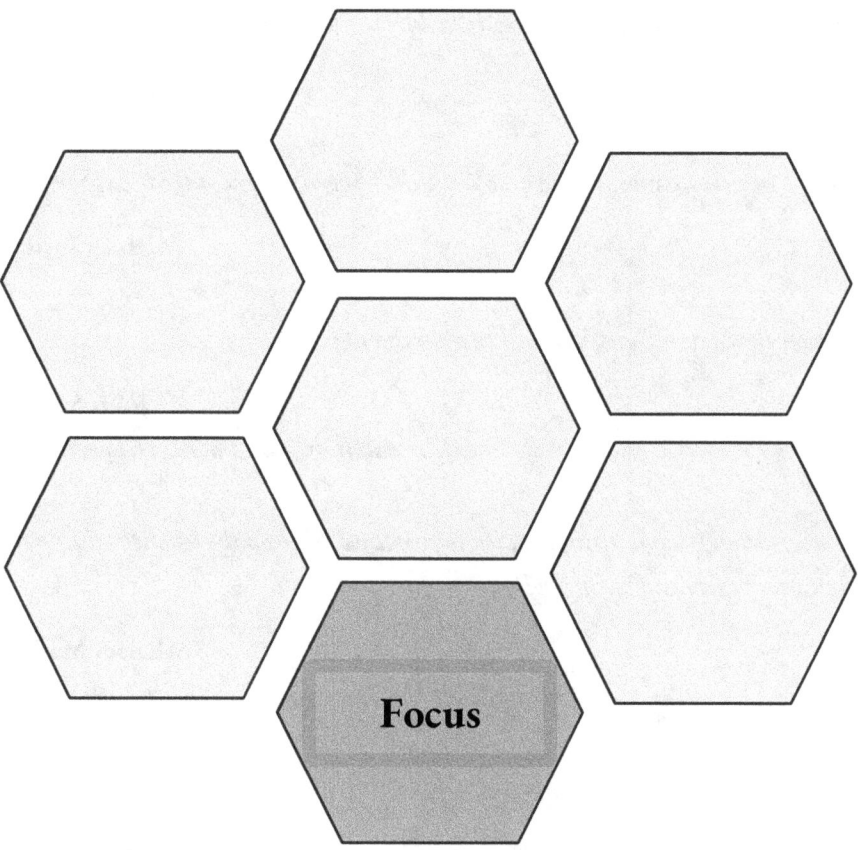

Focus

If you lose hope, somehow you lose that vitality that keeps life moving, you lose that courage to be, that quality that helps you go on in spite of all. And so today I still have a dream.

Martin Luther King, Jr.

Courage is the most important of all the virtues because without courage, you can't practice any other virtue consistently.

Maya Angeıou

Some want it to happen, some wish it would happen, others make it happen.

Michaeı Jordan

If you can learn to focus, you will be a persistent person.

John Martin
Author, The Power of Persistence

Conversation is what ultimately led to people walking on the moon, building the first skyscraper, and curing polio.

Michaeı Mather
Author, Having Nothing, Possessing Everything

What gets measured gets managed.

Peter Drucker
To assess meaningfully, we have to name what matters.

Success is the sum of small efforts, repeated day in and day out.

Robert Coııier
Persistent progress isn't flashy—it's stacked effort over time.

You cannot improve what you do not measure.

James Clear
Honest assessment is a mirror, not a judgment.

Not everything that can be counted counts, and not everything that counts can be counted.

William Bruce Cameron (often misattributed to Einstein)
A reminder to include intangibles—
like trust, morale, or courage.

Celebrate what you've accomplished, but raise the bar a little higher each time you succeed.

Mia Hamm
Reflection isn't just looking back—
it's fuel for moving forward.

The true measure of your success is how many times you can bounce back from failure.

Stephen Richards
In long efforts, resilience is part of what you've achieved.

Are we being effective, or just busy?

Unknown
A crucial question for assessing impact over activity.

Progress is not in enhancing what is, but in advancing toward what will be.

Khalil Gibran
Keep your assessment focused on the trajectory,
not just the present.

Judge your success by what you had to give up in order to get it.

Daıai Lama
A deeper lens: What was the cost of the accomplishment?

The journey is the reward.

Taoist Proverb
***In persistent efforts, the process itself is
often the truest accomplishment.***

*Courage is the most important of all the virtues because without courage, you
can't practice any other virtue consistently.*

Maya Angeıou

Some want it to happen, some wish it would happen, others make it happen.

Michaeı Jordan

*If you lose hope, somehow you lose that vitality that keeps life moving, you lose that
courage to be, that quality that helps you go on in spite of all. And so today I still
have a dream.*

Martin Luther King, Jr.

*Consider the postage stamp: its usefulness consists in the ability to stick to one
thing till it gets there.*

Josh Bıııings

*The difference between perseverance and obstinacy is that one comes from a strong
will, and the other from a strong won't.*

Henry Ward Beecher

Perseverance is a great element of success. If you only knock long enough at the gate, you are sure to wake up somebody.

Henri Wadsworth Longfellow

People always tell me, "Oh, you're such a good hitter!" They forget the 10,000 hours I spent out on the field practicing.

Ted Williams
***Baseball All-Star and considered one of
the greatest players in the game.***

No great achievement is possible without persistent work.

Bertrand Russell

You are capable of more than you know. Choose a goal that seems right for you and strive to be the best, however hard the path. Aim high. Behave honorably. Prepare to be alone at times, and to endure failure. Persist! The world needs all you can give.

E. O. Wilson

There is always a large horizon.... There is much to be done. It is up to you to contribute some small part to a program of human betterment for all time.

Francis Perkins
***Served as Secretary of Labor under President Franklin
Roosevelt and was the driving force behind the Social
Security Act legislation passed in 1935***

Do not fear mistakes. You will know failure. Continue to reach out.

Benjamin Franklin

My biggest failure was in business. I lost humbleness. When you have achieved success you get excited and lose insight into the future. You start to go downhill. You need to stay humble.

Hidehiko Yuzaki
Governor of Hiroshima Prefecture, Japan

I don't think about [failure].

Andy Rachieff
Lecturer and Cofounder, Wealthfront Inc

...Ignore that impulse and keep plugging. You're closer than you realize to accessing your inner innovator.

Tom Jacobs

Go out on a limb. That's where the fruit is.

Jimmy Carter
39th President of the United States

The Lord gave us two ends: one to sit on and the other to think with. Success depends on which one we use the most.

Ann Landers
A renowned columnist who started in 1955 and for nearly five decades provided advice to solitary souls in search of solutions

Stronger than all the armies is an idea whose time has come.

Victor Hugo

Never follow someone else's path. Unless you're in the woods and you're lost and you see a path, then by all means you should follow that.

Ellen DeGeneres

...AND...

In the off-chance you are having a difficult time with "focus," consider this thought...

All I ever wanted was to make a difference, travel the world, meet interesting people, find the missing link, fight the good fight, live for the moment, seize each day, make a fortune, know what really matters, end world hunger, befriend the dragon, be super popular but too cool to care, be master of my own fate, embrace my destiny, feel as much as I can feel, give too much, and love everything.

Tatsuya Ishida
A Japanese-American known for his ongoing satire and irreverent humor on a wide range of life topics. His statement is the essence of FOMO, or Fear Of Missing Out

Assess

Assessing accomplishments in a persistent journey is powerful. It's not just about checking boxes; it's about noticing progress, *alignment*, and *impact*—even in small wins. Here are some quotes that reflect on how we view achievement, particularly in the context of long-term, purpose-driven efforts...

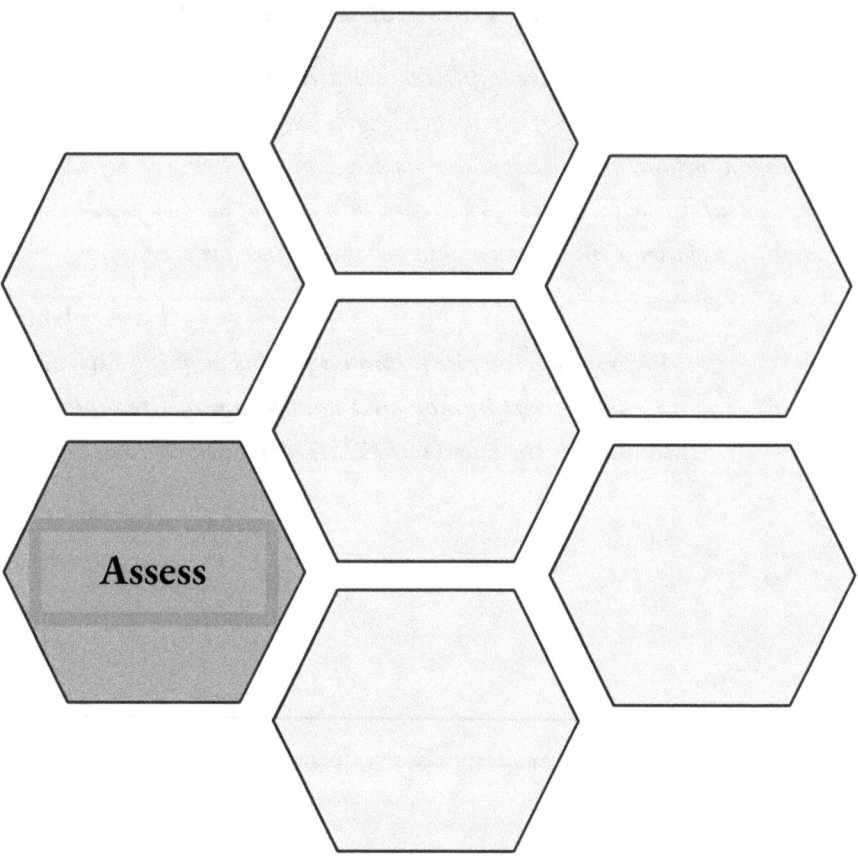

Every adversity, every failure, every heartache carries with it the seed of an equal or greater benefit.

Franklin Delano Roosevelt, 32nd President of the United States
A statement upon signing the unemployment insurance aid to house children, maternal and child welfare, and public health services programs

Practice does make perfect. Perfect practice makes perfect.

Anaudin
Former in-house composer for the Stan Kenton Orchestra Co-founder of Second City and well-known Pianist, Teacher, Composer

I used to think the point was to learn a piece and play it perfectly. But then, it occurred to me that it's not the point. The point is to learn what the piece wants to teach me.

Karen Dodson
An elder piano student who started playing as a young child, pursued a career, forgot about music, and regained her interest after retiring from her career.

Success is a journey, and hard work is the path to follow.

Anonymous Fortune Cookie Advice
Offered following a dinner upon completing the "X+" draft of The Persistence Factor

Success is almost totally dependent upon drive and persistence. The extra energy required to make another effort or try another approach is the secret of winning.

Denis Waitley

Perseverance is the hard work you do after you get tired of doing the hard work you already did.

Newt Gingrich
Former Member of U.S. Congress

The best way to assess yourself is to base the assessment on the product you produce daily.

Sunday Adelaia

Without proper self-evaluation, failure is inevitable.

John Wooden

You only live once, but if you do it right, once is enough.

Mae West

Thinking rationally is often different from "positive thinking," in that it is a realistic assessment of the situation, with a view towards rectifying the problem if possible.

Albert Ellis

Live as if you were to die tomorrow. Learn as if you were to live forever.

Mahatma Gandhi

One should be able to see that things are hopeless and yet be determined to make them otherwise.

F. Scott Fitzgerald

Lord, I hate buttermilk. Lord, I hate lard. And, Lord, you know I don't much care for raw white flour. But Lord, when you mix them all together and bake them, I do love warm fresh biscuits. So Lord, when things come up that we don't like, when life gets hard, when we don't understand what you're saying to us, help us to just relax and wait until you are done mixing. It will probably be even better than biscuits. Amen!

Oiivia Castro
A dear friend of the author who shared this prayer that is often used in religious settings to encourage persistence, patience and trust.

Hope is like a path in the countryside. Originally, there is nothing – but as people walk this way again and again, a path appears.

Lu Xun
Chinese Writer

Integration

INTEGRATION is a powerful phase of any persistent journey where you assess what you've learned so you can become wiser, stronger, and more effective. Integration is what transforms mistakes into insight, and effort into evolution...

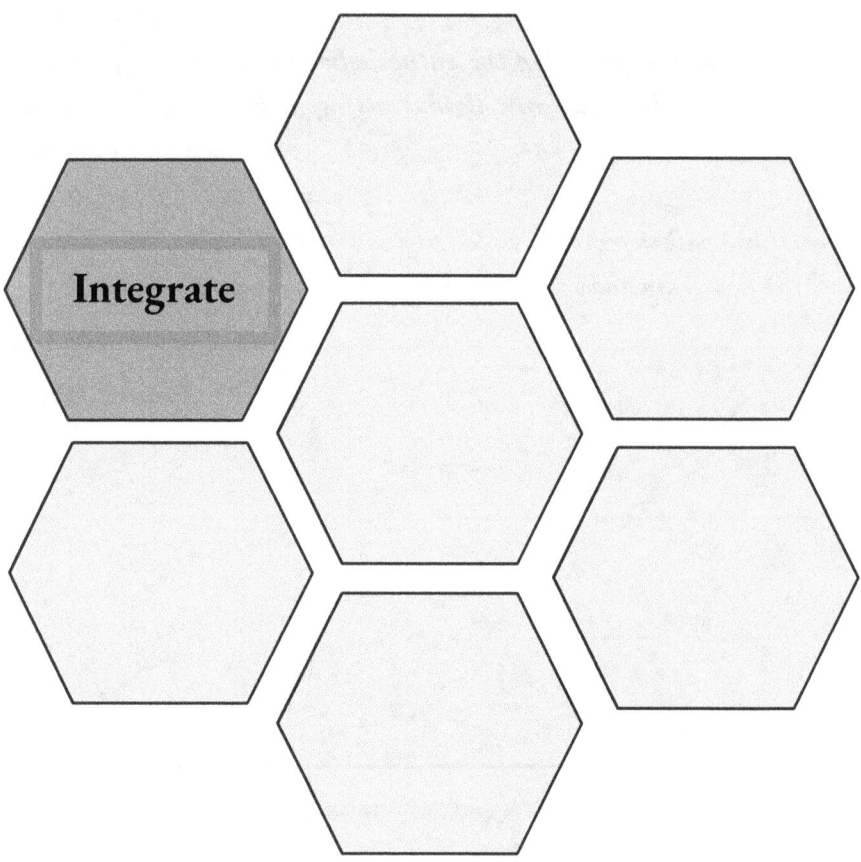

We do not learn from experience... we learn from reflecting on experience.

John Dewey
Reflection is the bridge from doing to understanding.

Good judgment comes from experience, and a lot of that comes from bad judgement.

Wiɪɪ Rogers
On the other hand, understanding can evolve from bad experiences as well

The lesson you struggle with will repeat itself until you learn it.

Unknown
Integration is how you break the loop and move forward.

In every success story, you will find someone who made a courageous decision.

Peter F. Drucker
Learning only becomes transformation when it leads to new action.

Take the best. Leave the rest. Learn the lesson.

Unknown
A clean framework for processing even tough or messy experiences

Failure is only the opportunity to begin again, this time more intelligently.

Henry Ford
Real persistence is adaptive, not stubborn.

Knowledge is of no value unless you put it into practice.

Anton Chekhov
***Integration means doing differently
based on what you've learned.***

The past is your lesson. The present is your gift. The future is your motivation.

Zig Zigıar
***Learning fuels the momentum that carries persistence
forward.***

Character consists of what you do on the third and fourth tries.

James   **A.**   **Michener**

Wisdom is not a product of schooling but of the lifelong attempt to acquire it.

Aıbert Einstein
Persistence is a learning posture, not just a goal.

*It's not about having the right opportunities. It's about handling the
opportunities right.*

Mark Hunter
Integration = skillful response, not just raw effort

Success is stumbling from failure to failure with no loss of enthusiasm.

AND

*Socialism is a philosophy of failure, the creed of ignorance, and the gospel of envy,
its inherent virtue is the equal sharing of misery.*

Sir Winston Churchiıı
Prime Minister of England during WWII

When you know better, you do better.

Maya Angelou
This is the spirit of integration: evolve with grace.

If the fool would persist in his folly he would become wise.

William Blake

Failure is the condiment that gives success its flavor.

Truman Capote

We are made to persist. That's how we find out who we are.

Tobias Wolff

The man who can drive himself further once the effort gets painful is the man who will win.

Roger Bannister

Figuring out the balance of work and family and personal time. It's a struggle. I tend to be heavily weighted in two of those things and the third falls by the wayside.

Jeff Fluhr
CEO, Spreecast

Great things are done by a series of small things brought together.

Vincent van Gogh

Mistakes are the portals of discovery.

James Joyce

A real failure is when you make a mistake and don't do the right thing, fix it as quickly as you can, own it, and learn from it.

Beth Cross, CEO
Ariat International

Nothing ever goes away until it has taught us what we need to know.

Pema Chodron

Winning is great, sure, but if you are really going to do something in life, the secret is learning how to lose. Nobody goes undefeated all the time. If you can pick up after a crushing defeat, and go on to win again, you are going to be a champion someday.

Wilma Rudolph

Live the life you've always dreamed of. Be fearless in the face of adversity. Never stop learning. Use your imagination whenever possible. Recognize the beauty that surrounds you. Remember where you came from, but never lose sight of where you are going.

Frequently attributed to Les Brown, Motivational Speaker
...but actually derived from an Unknown Source
A summation of summations

I like to consider failures "noble experiments."

Chip Conley, Founder of Joie de Vivre Hotels

The season of failure is the best time for sowing the seeds of success.

Paramahansa Yogananda

You make mistakes. Mistakes don't make you.

Maxwell Maltz

Do not brood over your past mistakes and failures as this will only fill your mind with grief, regret and depression. Do not repeat them in the future.

Swami Sivananda

I have made mistakes, but I don't feel I need to look at life and say, "That was a failure" or "That was a success." I don't believe in using that language. We are all doing our best.

Jessica Jackley
Cofounder of Kiva

Failure is the key to success; each mistake teaches us something.

Morihei Ueshiba

Patience, persistence and perspiration make an unbeatable combination for success.

AND

Before success comes in any man's life, he's sure to meet with much temporary defeat and, perhaps some failures. When defeat overtakes a man, the easiest and the most logical thing to do is to quit. That's exactly what the majority of men do.

AND

The three great essentials to achieve anything worthwhile are, first, hard work; second, stick-to-itiveness; third, common sense.

AND

Many of life's failures are people who did not realize how close they were to success when they gave up.

AND

Patience, persistence and perspiration make an unbeatable combination for success.

AND

Before success comes in any man's life, he's sure to meet with much temporary defeat and, perhaps some failures. When defeat overtakes a man, the easiest and the most logical thing to do is to quit. That's exactly what the majority of men do.

Napoleon Hill
Author and advocate who believes fervent expectations are essential to improving one's life.

I have missed more than 9,000 shots in my career. I have lost almost 300 games. On 26 occasions, I have been entrusted to take the game-winning shot, and I missed. I have failed over and over and over again in my life. And that is why I succeed.

AND

I've failed over and over and over again in my life. And that is why I succeed.

Michael Jordan
Considered one of the very best basketball players in history, but who did not make his high school basketball team, went on to lead the field.

I have not failed. I've just found 10,000 ways that do not work."

Thomas Edison
His teachers at school described him as "too stupid to learn anything" because of his hearing impairment, but his Mom

knew differently...so she "home-schooled" him, and he went
on to invent the light bulb via the route of persistence.

Better a spectacular failure, than a benign success.

Malcolm McLaren

Rather than jumping over someone to get what you want, consider reaching out your hand and taking the leap side by side, because life is better when we leap together.

Kermit the Frog
In a commencement speech to the University of Maryland graduation class, 2025

I can do things you cannot, you can do things I cannot; together, we can do great things.

Mother Teresa
A widely recognized quote that represented her core philosophy of life and the need for working together

Together, we can change the world – one heart, one life, one moment of awakening at a time.

Ben Keesey
Director of Development for the Center for Action and Contemplation, Founded by Father Richard Rohr

Try again. Fail again. Fail better.

Samuel Beckett

High moral and ethical standards are essential, and they don't change from one job to another, or from one level of authority to another. Honesty, truthfulness, integrity, unselfishness – these are always there. And whenever a leader violates these basic principles, through arrogance or through ignorance, there's a derogation of duty.

Jimmy Carter
39th President of the United States in an interview with the Harvard Business Review, March 1988

Next to excellence is the appreciation of it.

William Makepeace Thackeray
From an article in Forbes Magazine

We may encounter many defeats, but we must never be defeated.

Maya Angelou
One of the most thoughtful people we should all listen to...

Alone, we can do so little; together we can do so much.

Helen Keller

Sticks in a bundle are unbreakable.

Anonymous

My humanity is bound up in yours, for we can only be human together.

Bishop Desmond Tutu

And, Finally, Persistence

PERSISTENCE is the fuel behind every meaningful change, every breakthrough, every purpose-driven life. The following words have carried people through hardship, doubt, and delay with courage and clarity...

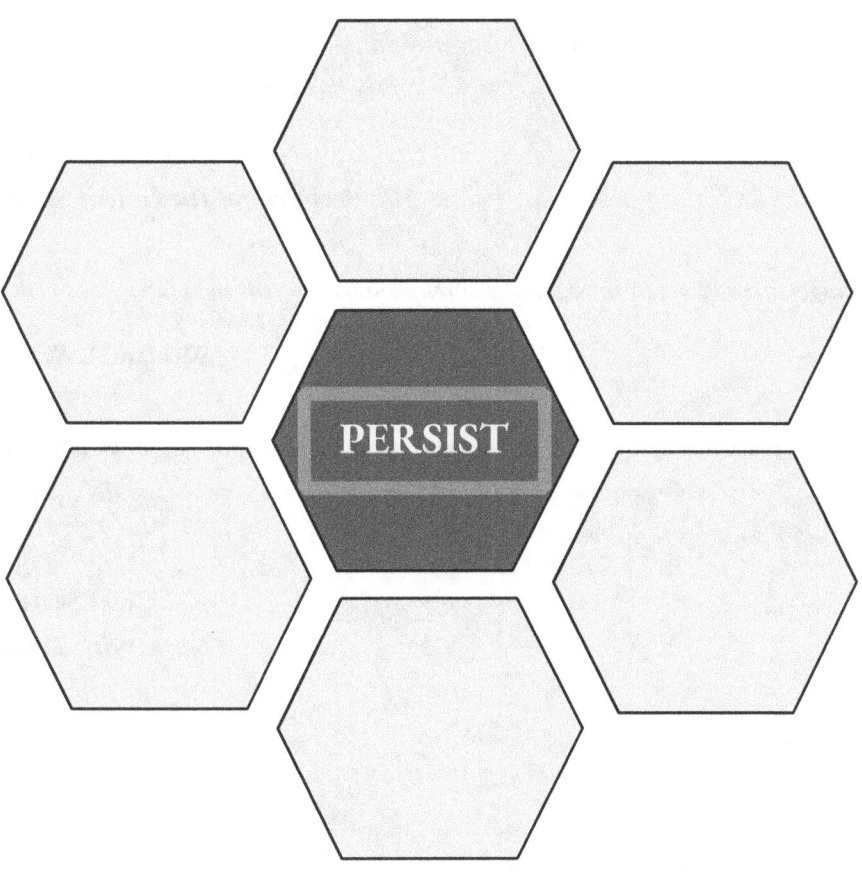

PERSIST

Nothing in the world can take the place of Persistence. Talent will not; nothing is more common than unsuccessful men with talent. Genius will not; unrewarded genius is almost a proverb. Education will not; the world is full of educated derelicts. Persistence and determination alone are omnipotent. The slogan 'Press On' has solved and always will solve the problems of the human race.

AND

Persistence and determination alone are omnipotent. The slogan 'press on' has solved and always will solve the problems of the human race.

Calvin Coolidge
30*^h* President of the United States

Judge each day not by the harvest you reap but by the seeds you plant.

William A. Ward

When you know who you are; when your mission is clear and you burn with the inner fire of unbreakable will; no cold can touch your heart; no deluge can dampen your purpose. You know that you are alive.

Chief Seattle
Duwamish Tribe

Never give up! Never! Never! Never!

AND

Success is not final, failure is not fatal: It is the courage to continue that counts.

Sir Winston Churchill
**Prime Minister of England during WWII on persistence,
carrying you through the middle**

The key of persistence opens all doors closed by resistance.

John Di Lemme

Knowing trees, I understand the meaning of patience. Knowing grass, I can appreciate persistence.

Hal Borland
Naturalist and Author

That's one small step for man, and one giant leap for mankind.

Neil Armstrong
In stepping out of his capsule on the moon on July 20, 1969

Not everything that is faced can be changed but nothing can be changed until it is faced.

James Baldwin

I have not failed. I've just found 10,000 ways that won't work.

Thomas A. Edison

It always seems impossible until it's done.

Nelson Mandela
Persistence is about pushing through the illusion of impossibility.

Energy and persistence conquer all things.

Benjamin Franklin
A steady flame, not a flash fire.

Fall seven times, stand up eight.

Japanese Proverb
A beautiful, simple image of resilient persistence.

Perseverance is not a long race; it is many short races one after the other.

Waiter Eniot
Persistence is a daily rhythm, not a one-time decision.

Most of the important things in the world have been accomplished by people who kept on trying when there seemed to be no hope at all.

Daie Carnegie
Persistence births possibility.

The difference between a successful person and others is not a lack of strength or knowledge, but rather a lack of will.

Vince Lombardi
Willpower—sustained—makes the difference.

Ambition is the path to success. Persistence is the vehicle you arrive in.

Senator Biu Bradiey
It's not just about dreaming—it's about driving.

You just can't beat the person who never gives up.

Babe Ruth
Simple. Ruthless. True.

The drops of rain make a hole in the stone not by violence but by often falling.

Lucretius

I'm going to do something until I get it right.

Giannis Antetokounmpo
Forward for the Milwaukee Bucks

In the confrontation between the stream and the rock, the stream always wins - not through strength, but through persistence.

Buddha

Success if the result of perfection, hard work, learning from failure, loyalty, and persistence.

Colin Powell
Former Secretary of State

You can count on the fact that you are going to take a blow here and there and, you just have to keep rolling the rock back up the hill. It's about perseverance.

Miles White
Former CEO, Abbott Lab

First, say to yourself what you would be, and then do what you have to do.

AND

Tentative effort leads to tentative outcomes.

Epictetus
Philosopher in the Greek Stoic Tradition

Ever tried. Ever failed. No matter. Try again. Fail again. Fail better.

Samuel Beckett

We must have perseverance and, above all, confidence in ourselves. We must believe that we are gifted for something and that this thing must be attained.

Marie Curie

There is no elevator to success; you have to take the stairs.

Zig Ziglar

The solution to every problem is simple. It's the distance between the two where the mystery lies.

Derek Landy
Irish author best known for the Skulduggery Pleasant series

Persistence is the most powerful force on earth, it can move mountains.

Albert Einstein

It's not where you go but, who you go with.

Charles Schultz
Creator of the Peanuts cartoon series

Always end the day with a positive thought. No matter how hard today was, tomorrow is full of possibilities.

Unknown Author

I never quit until I get what I'm after and that's the only difference between me, that's supposed to be lucky and the fellows that think they are unlucky.

Thomas Edison

...AND...

Final Thoughts From The Author

The downside of persistence is not taking sufficient time to learn and digest your failures, to move on too quickly without considering how you got to where you are.

AND

Persistence is not a solo enterprise. In fact, the true power of persistence is when others join you in reaching your objective.

AND

The downside of persistence is not taking sufficient time to learn and digest your failures. To move on too quickly without considering what could have ...what should have been done differently in pursuit of your goal.

Kevin Fickenscher
Author, The Persistence Factor

Notes

[1] The Fickenscher Files. https://www.thecreonetwork.com/follow-creo/our-blog

[2] In French, meaning "to persist" or "continue."

[3] In French, meaning "to insist or to persevere."

[4] International Churchill Society. (1941, October 20). *Never Give In Audio*. https://winstonchurchill.org/resources/speeches/1941-1945-war-leader/never-give-in-audio/

[5] American Psychological Association. *Resilience*. https://www.apa.org/topics/resilience

[6] Microbiology, Physiology, Pharmacology, PickYourFavorite-ology

[7] A paraphrase of Lewis Carroll's "*Alice's Adventures in Wonderland*", Chapter 6: "Would **you** tell me, please, which way I ought to **go** from here?"

[8] Wikipedia. *Calvin Coolidge*. https://en.wikipedia.org/wiki/Calvin_Coolidge

[9] While Gene Kranz is often identified as the source of the quote, he actually did not say it but only indicated to the producers of "Apollo 13" the movie that the NASA team did not consider "failure" when problems occurred. Rather, it was inserted as a statement by the producers of the movie and later adopted as a book title by Mr. Kranz.

[10] https://www.womenshistory.org

[11] Adapted from All Time Short Stories, http://alltimeshortstories.com/purpose-of-life/

[12] Friedrich Nietzsche, *Twilight of the Idols (1895)* – Maxims #12, Chapter 1 "Maxims and Arrows".

[13] https://www.themyersbriggs.com

[14] www.capt.org

[15] https://www.discprofile.com

[16] If you're following the narrative, you will recall my session with Mom over the fact that I should pursue medicine rather than acting. In retrospect, I suspect she may have talked with Mr. Moreland to gain his support since the discussion with him came shortly after Mom's intervention.

[17] https://www.merriam-webster.com/dictionary/nudge

[18] Thaler & Sunstein, 2008, p.6.

[19] https://hr.utexas.edu/manager/tools/mentoring

[20] Wikipedia. *Nelson Mandela.* https://en.wikipedia.org/wiki/Nelson_Mandela

[21] The demographic cohort of people born primarily between 1901 and 1927, who experienced the Great Depression and fought in World War II, often characterized by their resilience, patriotism, and commitment to hard work due to the challenges they faced during their youth; the term was popularized by journalist Tom Brokaw in his book "The Greatest Generation."

[22] Skills You Need. *Building Confidence.* https://www.skillsyouneed.com/ps/confidence.html

[23] *The strength of persistence and the power of focus.* https://steemit.com/motivation/@nphacker/the-strength-of-persistence-and-the-power-of-focus

[24] Chew. L. (2017, May 7). *Don't focus on your situation, focus on your trajectory.* Medium. https://medium.com/the-mission/dont-focus-on-your-situationn-focus-on-your-trajectory-27713f0ce175

[25] Source: Unknown

[26] Minnesota Brain Injury Alliance. *Veterans and brain inury-Personal stories.* https://www.braininjurymn.org/veterans/stories-p1.php

[27] McBean, B. (2013, January 24). *The 5 characteristics of great leaders.* Fast Company. https://www.fastcompany.com/3004914/5-characteristics-great-leaders

[28] The Obama White House. (2012, December 14). *President Obama makes a statement on the shooting in Newtown, Connecticut.* YouTube. https://www.youtube.com/watch?v=mIA0W69U2_Y

[29] Trump White House Archived. (2018, February 15). *President Trump delivers remarks on the tragedy in Parkland, FL.* YouTube. https://www.youtube.com/watch?v=GFHvpYbe41U

[30] Wikipedia. *Bodhicitta.* https://en.wikipedia.org/wiki/Bodhicitta

[31] Brown, B., (2012). *Daring greatly: How the courage to be vulnerable transforms the way we live, love, parent and lead.* Gotham Books.

[32] Valis, D., Bartlett, L.M.. (2010, March). The Failure Phenomenon: A Critique. *International Journal of Performability Engineering,* Volume 6, Number 2. Paper 7, pp. 181-190.

[33] Edmonson, A. (2011, April). *Strategies for learning from failure.* Harvard Business Review. https://hbr.org/2011/04/strategies-for-learning-from-failure

[34] Millard, C. (2005). *The river of doubt: Theodore Roosevelt's darkest journey.* First Anchor Books.

[35] Millard, C. (2005). *The river of doubt: Theodore Roosevelt's darkest journey*. First Anchor Books. P.38

[36] Weinzimmer, L., McConoughey, J. (2012). The wisdom of failure: How to learn the tough leadership lessons without paying the price. Jossey-Bass.

[37] Edmonson, A. (2011, April). *Strategies for learning from failure*. Harvard Business Review. https://hbr.org/2011/04/strategies-for-learning-from-failure

[38] Kolb, D. A. (1984). *Experiential learning: Experience as the source of learning and development*. Englewood Cliffs, NJ: Prentice Hall.

[39] From an email sent to the author by a colleague, *S.Koch, in 2017*.

[40] Deutschendorf, H. 7 Habits of highly persistent people. The Teen Mentor. https://theteenmentor.com/2019/02/18/7-habits-of-highly-persistent-people-by-harvey-deutschendorf/

[41] There are multiple incidents like this situation.

[42] For additional detail: Stawicki, E. (2007, August 2). *Why did the I35-W bridge collapse?* MPR News. https://www.mprnews.org/story/2007/08/02/bridgehistory

[43] Wikipedia. *Peter Drucker*. https://en.wikipedia.org/wiki/Peter_Drucker

[44] Society for Health Resource Management offers the following details for failure resolution: https://www.shrm.org/resourcesandtools/hr-topics/employee-relations/pages/10-tips-for-changing-your-companys-culture%E2%80%94and-making-it-stick.aspx

[45] Wikipedia. *Fundamental attribution error*. https://en.wikipedia.org/wiki/Fundamental_attribution_error

[46] Wikipedia. *Space Shuttle Columbia Disaster*. https://en.wikipedia.org/wiki/Space_Shuttle_Columbia_disaster

[47] https://www.moreincommon.com

[48] http://digitalexhibits.libraries.wsu.edu/exhibits/show/2016sphist417/immigration/germans-and-scandinavians

[49] NOTE: At the time, farmers were entirely dependent upon the vagaries of the weather patterns. Today, the Ogallala Aquifer provides a regular resources for irrigation, although the aquifer is increasingly in trouble because the irrigation has exceeded the resupply in most years for the last three quarters of a century.

[50] Westcott, N. E. (2011). The prolonged 1954 midwestern US heat wave: Impacts and responses. *Weather, Climate, and Society, 3*(3), 165-176. https://journals.ametsoc.org/doi/pdf/10.1175/WCAS-D-10-05002.1

[51] Adapted from an article by John Steinbreder, *Fortune Magazine,* June 6, 1988.

[52] S. Sitkin, Learning through failure: the strategy of small losses, in L. L. Cummings and B. Staw (eds.), *Research in Organizational Behavior 14,* JAI Press, Greenwich, CT, 231e266 (1992).

[53] *Sharing Buddhist practice*. Bear River Meditation Group. https://bearrivermeditationgroup.wordpress.com/2012/02/20/the-tea-ceremony-by-thich-nhat-hanh/

[54] Wikipedia. *Forgiveness*. https://en.wikipedia.org/wiki/Forgiveness

[55] An ongoing comment from my personal mentor when he offered an observation that others failed to point out.

[56] Loretto, P. (Updated 2024, September 9). *What qualities make a good mentor?* The Balance. https://www.thebalance.com/qualities-of-a-good-mentor-1986663 - NOTE: I have used the term "reliable" instead of "good" because of the need for consistent and ongoing guidance, assistance, and mentoring to effective support the individual pursuing the path of *The Persistence Factor*.

[57] Notable from the "the last century" because of their actual accomplishment could not have occurred without wide national or international support as well as the fact that both examples represent the essence of persistence.

[58] In 2018, I was attending a conference on the Big Island of Hawaii, when such an alert was announced as we were walking to our lectures for the day. Again, an unforgettable situation as we huddled in the laundry room of this gigantic hotel with the hotel staff standing in a prayer circle offering prayers as the announcements blurted out warnings over the loudspeaker of a "potential" incoming nuclear missile. Meanwhile, one of our friends went out to the beach to watch the possible incoming.

[59] **An anecdote to share:** I will never forget the SALT agreement where Presidents Reagan and Gorbachev met in Reykjavik, Iceland. As a Kellogg Fellow, I was visiting Ecuador, and our group happened to be up in the Andes visiting a small, rural town for a "community meeting". We were gathered in a small house, all cramped together. As we opened the meeting, one of our members asked if the assembled had any particular issues they wanted to discuss. The interpreters fielded the question in multiple languages. In the back of the room, a gentleman quickly raised his hand and asked a question in a dialect from the Amazon, which was interpreted into the contemporary Native dialect, which was then translated into Spanish and finally into English. And the question was: "What results did we expect from the Reagan-Gorbachev discussion at the SALT meeting and was there hope now possible for the rest of the world to avoid a nuclear war?" Remember: Up in the Andes, miles and miles from any type of communication infrastructure,

translating through four languages. Need I say more about "reaching out" to gain support for a cause?

[60] Begay, M. – a legacy story from the Navajo people on the state of leadership for their nation.